Christianity
EXPLORED

One life. What's it all about?

Christianity Explored Leader's Guide (3rd Edition)
Copyright © 2011 Christianity Explored
First published in 2011. Reprinted 2011, 2012 (twice), 2014

www.ceministries.org

Published by
The Good Book Company Ltd
Blenheim House, 1 Blenheim Road, Epsom, Surrey, KT19 9AP, UK
Tel: 0333-123-0880; International: +44 (0) 208 942 0880
Email: admin@thegoodbook.co.uk

Websites:
UK and Europe: www.thegoodbook.co.uk
North America: www.thegoodbook.com
Australia: www.thegoodbook.com.au
New Zealand: www.thegoodbook.co.nz

CHRISTIANITY
EXPLORED
MINISTRIES

ISBN: 9781907377587

Design by Steve Devane and André Parker

Printed in the Czech Republic

Introduction

When we first started running *Christianity Explored* fifteen years ago at All Souls, Langham Place in London, we were uncertain how it would be received.

We were pretty sure that opening up the message of Jesus by walking through the Gospel of Mark would be a great thing to do. But we have been amazed by how God has honoured and blessed this simple approach to outreach.

We are so thankful that, since those early days, hundreds of thousands of people throughout the world have encountered the real Jesus as he walks off the pages of Scripture. The course has stimulated thought and discussion – and people have been challenged to consider the claim of Christ on their lives. *Christianity Explored* has been translated into over 20 languages and continues to grow.

What makes this course – and the Christian gospel – distinctive is its insistence on God's remarkable grace: the clear teaching that although we have rebelled against God, we are deeply loved by him. Loved with an outrageous, costly and incomprehensible love that was poured out for us on a little hill just outside Jerusalem.

This third edition has been reworked as a seven-session course. With a creative mixture of Bible studies, talks, DVDs, group discussions and home Bible-reading, group members will discover the identity, mission and call of Jesus – who Jesus is, what he came to do, and how he calls us to respond.

And you are an important part in bringing this good news to your friends, family or neighbourhood. Trust in the Holy Spirit's power to open blind eyes, because this ancient story with its many life-changing truths will find its way into the hearts and souls of those who hear it. And by the miracle of God's grace, you will be part of others coming to know the love and salvation that only Christ can give.

If you are running a *Christianity Explored* course, please register it on our website **www.ceministries.org**, so that we and others can pray for you, or even send other people along.

May God richly bless you in all you do with this course for the honour and glory of Christ.

Rico Tice, Barry Cooper, Craig Dyer
and the Christianity Explored Team, February 2011

Section 2: Study guide   67

Section 3: Day away   129

Appendices   151

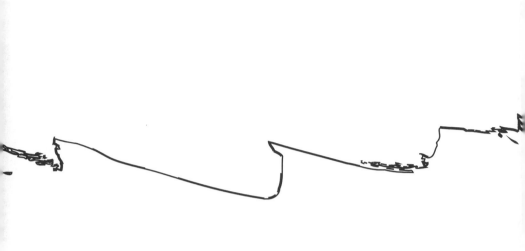

How to run the course

Two *Christianity Explored* websites to help you:

www.christianityexplored.org
This website is for non-Christians, whether or not they are on a course. It features a visual gospel outline based on the Gospel of Mark, answers to common questions, and testimonies from a wide variety of people, as well as information about the *Christianity Explored* course. You can find more details at the back of this book, on page 255.

www.ceministries.org
For leaders looking for information, downloads and resources.

And to order resources:
www.thegoodbook.co.uk • www.thegoodbook.com
www.thegoodbook.com.au • www.thegoodbook.co.nz
Visit your local Good Book website for everything you need to run a *Christianity Explored* course – including invitations, posters, handbooks and DVDs. You can also download digital episodes of the CE video material in SD and HD format.

Getting started

Telling people about Jesus Christ is a stunning privilege and a huge responsibility. It's a stunning privilege because Almighty God is pleased to call us his "fellow workers" (1 Corinthians 3:9) as he seeks and saves the lost. And it's a huge responsibility because it can be tempting to present a watered-down gospel that has no power to save and is "no gospel at all" (Galatians 1:7). Our evangelism must always be careful, prayerful and faithful.

Christianity Explored has been developed to let the gospel tell the gospel: it takes your group members on a seven-session journey through Mark's Gospel to discover who Jesus is, why he came and what it means to follow him.

To help your journey run smoothly, you will need to consider the following before the course begins.

STRUCTURE OF THE COURSE

How and when you meet will depend on your situation. Many courses run on a midweek evening for seven weeks, with a day away on the Saturday between sessions six and seven. But your circumstances may be different. Eg:

- a daytime women's group

- a fortnightly home group

- a church houseparty

- a Sunday group running at the same time as the regular church service

- a college Christian Union or fellowship

- a few people meeting round a kitchen table

The course material can be adapted to suit your situation, including meeting one-to-one with a friend or neighbour. However, you will find it helpful to meet as regularly as possible – and please don't skip any sessions or change the order (including using the day away material between sessions six and seven).

The chart on the next page shows how the course is structured, and how the themes fit together.

	Session	Explore (Bible study)	Listen (Talk/DVD)	Discuss	Follow up (at home)
Identity	**Session 1** What are we doing here? *We're here to explore the good news about Jesus Christ.*	Welcome	Good news	Discuss talk/DVD	Mark 1:1 – 3:6
Identity	**Session 2** Who is Jesus? *Jesus is the Christ (God's only chosen King) and God's Son.*	Mark 4:35-41	Identity	Discuss talk/DVD	Mark 3:7 – 5:43
Mission	**Session 3** Why did Jesus come? *Jesus came to cure our heart problem – our sin.*	Mark 2:1-12	Sin	Discuss talk/DVD	Mark 6:1 – 8:29
Mission	**Session 4** Why did Jesus die? *Jesus died to rescue us from sin, by taking the punishment we deserve.*	Mark 8:22-33	The cross	Discuss talk/DVD	Mark 8:30 – 10:52
Mission	**Session 5** Why did Jesus rise? *The resurrection proves that God accepted the ransom Jesus paid, that death has been beaten, and that Jesus will come back to judge everyone.*	Mark 14:27-31	Resurrection	Discuss talk/DVD	Mark 11:1 – 13:37
Call	**Session 6** How can God accept us? *God accepts us not because of anything we've done but because of what Jesus has done. This is grace – God's undeserved gift to us.*	Mark 10:13-16	Grace	Discuss talk/DVD	Mark 14:1 – 16:8

	Session	Explore (Bible study)	Listen (Talk/DVD)	Discuss	Follow up (at home)
Call	**Day away** **1:** Listen carefully *We must listen to Jesus, and act on what we hear.* **2:** Ask humbly *Following Jesus is about service, not status. We need to ask Jesus for mercy, not a reward.* **3:** Choose wisely *Ignoring Jesus' call to repent and believe will eventually earn us the rejection of Jesus.*	Mark 4:1-9 and 13-20	The sower James and John King Herod	Discuss talk/DVD	
Call	**Session 7** What does it mean to follow Jesus? *A follower of Jesus "must deny himself and take up his cross". But what is given up is nothing compared to what is gained.*	Mark 1:14-15	Come and die	Discuss talk/DVD	

The first five weeks focus on who Jesus is and why he came – his *identity* and *mission*. Then during the final two sessions and the day away the emphasis is on what it means to follow Jesus – his *call*. In particular course members will explore Jesus' words in Mark 8:34: "If anyone would come after me, he must deny himself and take up his cross and follow me".

STRUCTURE OF A SESSION

Below is the suggested structure for an evening session. See "During the course" on page 43 for a fuller description of each component. Of course, depending on your circumstances, you might want to change the exact times, or offer coffee and cake instead of a meal. Equally, you might want to run the course during the day if that is a more suitable time for those you're trying to reach.

6:30 p.m.	Leaders' prayer meeting
7:00 p.m.	Guests arrive for the meal
7:45 p.m.	Explore (Bible study)
8:05 p.m.	Listen (Talk/DVD)
8:30 p.m.	Discuss
9:00 p.m.	End of the evening – "One-to-One"

Note: All times are approximate. You can make certain sessions shorter or longer depending on your circumstances.

You can run *Christianity Explored* with Bible talks presented by the course leader or by using the course DVD, which is presented by Rico Tice, who works at All Souls Church, Langham Place in London.

If you decide to run the course with the talks, you will find talk outlines in the appendix on page 153. Delivering the talks yourself will lead to a more personal, more intimate experience for the group members. You can also download the talks as Word documents so that you can adapt them for your own situation. They are available from **www.ceministries.org**

If you decide to run the course with the DVD, please note that because it features on-screen Bible text, it is inadvisable to use the DVD with large groups unless you have access to a projection screen and projector.

WHERE SHOULD YOU MEET?

Many groups meet in their church premises. However you may like to experiment with some different locations. Avoid using a classroom, or somewhere that looks like one, so that people don't feel they are back in school. A small group could be held in someone's home, or a small meeting room. Or you may be able to hire a space in a local coffee shop. A larger group could meet in a community hall, sports centre or local adult education centre. It's important to choose a place where you are unlikely to be interrupted and where you will be able to meet for every session at the same time.

The aim is to create a relational environment where people can listen to the Bible teaching while they enjoy the warmth of Christian friendship so that they feel sufficiently relaxed to ask their questions and express their doubts and feelings.

SETTING UP YOUR VENUE

It is important that guests feel relaxed and welcome, and the way you set up your venue will help you achieve that. The physical environment where you run *Christianity Explored* can have a big impact on people's willingness to get involved in discussion, so be creative in the way you set up the room.

With a small group, arrange the room so that everyone can see each other. Be careful that the group leader isn't sitting with their back to a window, which can make it harder for people to see them clearly. Ask any helpers to sit among the group members rather than next to the group leader. If your small group needs to meet in a large room, try to use screens and furniture to make a smaller, more friendly space in one corner.

If you are using the course DVD, place the screen where everyone can see it easily, and where there will not be reflections (eg: from windows) obscuring the picture.

If there are a large number of leaders and guests, set up a number of tables around which different groups can sit. Because each group will be engaged in separate discussions, try to leave plenty of space between tables so that guests and leaders can hear each other easily.

- You will need a way of displaying visual aids (eg: PowerPoint, overhead projector or flipchart).

- You may like to set aside a table with a selection of books for guests and leaders to buy or borrow. (See **www.ceministries.org** for recommended books on various subjects.)

- If you are meeting in a large premises, make sure that facilities and exits are clearly marked.

Everyone involved in the course – leaders, guests and the course leader – will need a copy of Mark's Gospel or a Bible. It is important that everyone use the same version and edition so that page numbers will be the same. (The version used throughout the course material is the New International Version*.)

- Guests should each be given a Mark's Gospel or Bible at the beginning of the course, preferably one they can keep when the course ends.

- They should also be given a copy of the Handbook.

- Pens should be made available to allow guests to make notes or jot down questions.

- * **Note:** *Christianity Explored* uses the 1984 edition of the New International Version (NIV). The 2011 revised edition includes a number of changes to the English text in Mark's Gospel. Where these changes involve significant words or phrases that are used within the course, there are notes in this Leader's Guide to help you adapt the material if you are using the 2011 NIV.

Choosing and training leaders

If you have overall responsibility for running the course, you will need to choose and train leaders who will be responsible for those who attend.

CHOOSING LEADERS

Leaders should be mature Christians who are able to teach, encourage discussion and care for guests.

In selecting a leader, ask yourself: "Is this person able to teach the Bible faithfully and clearly? Will he or she be able to deal with difficult questions on Mark's Gospel?" (There is a section on answering questions from Mark in the appendix on page 237. This will help people as they prepare.)

Secondly, ask yourself: "Will this person be able to promote discussion without dominating it?" Since so much of the course revolves around discussion, guests need to feel free to be open and honest in their group.

Thirdly, ask yourself: "Is this the type of person who would make a guest feel welcome and cared for?" Rather than simply telling people about God's love, leaders must be willing to demonstrate that love by devoting time and attention to those in their care.

And of course, a leader's responsibility goes beyond seven sessions. Relationships begun during the course are likely to develop into friendships that must be nurtured once the course is over. For this reason, if possible, don't ask leaders to take on more than one course a year.

- A high ratio of leaders to group members is essential. For example, a well-balanced group may consist of two leaders and six guests, or three leaders and nine guests.

- If your course is likely to be large, make sure you have enough leaders, then divide them into teams of three.

- In order to deal with pastoral situations appropriately, it's advisable to assign a mixture of male and female leaders to each team.

List your leaders here.

TRAINING LEADERS

Training should take place before the course begins. Once a leader understands the reasoning behind *Christianity Explored*, it becomes much easier for him or her to commit the time required. As well as preparing leaders for the course, training together cements relationships between those who will be leading.

You should therefore include training before every course you run, and all leaders should be asked to attend – even if they have been leaders many times before. Feel free to vary the exercises so the training remains fresh for veteran leaders. Check **www.ceministries.org** for updates on training resources and opportunities.

The way you arrange the training will depend on your situation. You may choose to spend a day together, or two or three evenings, or meet early in the morning. There are some examples below of how you might schedule a training day or series of evenings.

There are eight short training modules, which start on page 27. They are designed so that they can be used in a group, as pairs, or by individuals. The ideal is to meet together for the reasons given above. However, if that isn't possible for some of your team, they can prepare for the course by working through the material themselves. It then becomes even more important that the whole team meet together before each session of the course starts so that they can discuss and pray together before the guests arrive.

- Ensure that every leader (including yourself) has a copy of this Leader's Guide, which contains the eight training modules.

- The modules should be read aloud by the person leading the training (often the course leader), allowing time for everyone to discuss and complete the exercises involved.

Example training day schedule

10:00 a.m.	Pray together	
10:15 a.m.	**Why evangelize?**	30 minutes
10:45 a.m.	**God's part in evangelism – and ours**	30 minutes
11:15 a.m.	**Being a Christianity Explored leader**	15 minutes
11:30 a.m.	**Before the course**	25 minutes
11:55 a.m.	Pray together	
12:00 p.m.	Lunch	
1:00 p.m.	**During the course**	60 minutes
2:00 p.m.	Coffee	
2:20 p.m.	**Identity, mission, call**	90 minutes
3:50 p.m.	Coffee	
4:10 p.m.	**After the course**	15 minutes
4:25 p.m.	**Getting our expectations right** 20 minutes	
4:45 p.m.	Pray together	

Example training schedule over three evenings

Evening 1

7:30 p.m.	Pray together	
7:45 p.m.	**Why evangelize?**	30 minutes
8:15 p.m.	**God's part in evangelism – and ours**	30 minutes
8:45 p.m.	**Being a Christianity Explored leader**	15 minutes
9:00 p.m.	**Before the course**	25 minutes
9:25 p.m.	Pray together	

Evening 2

7:30 p.m.	Pray together	
7:45 p.m.	**Identity, mission, call**	90 minutes
9:15 p.m.	Pray together	

Evening 3		
7:30 p.m.	**Pray together**	
7:45 p.m.	**During the course**	60 minutes
8:45 p.m.	**After the course**	15 minutes
9:00 p.m.	**Getting our expectations right**	20 minutes
9:20 p.m.	**Pray together**	

WELCOMING

The hardest part of *Christianity Explored* for many guests is getting through the door on the first night. This will be especially true if you're running your course in a church building, which for many will seem an unfamiliar, unwelcoming place.

One or more "welcomers" should be given the task of greeting people as they arrive. In a small group, these can be leaders who have been given a specific role of welcoming each arrival. In a larger group, choose welcomers who are not leaders: that way, leaders can concentrate on talking to guests who've already arrived. Leaders and welcomers should wear name tags so that they are immediately identifiable by guests.

When a guest arrives, welcomers should simply introduce themselves and find out the person's name. Asking for addresses or telephone numbers at this stage can make people feel uncomfortable. Take the guest to where the group will be meeting and introduce them to another leader. If your session is not including a meal, this would be a good time to offer people a drink (eg: tea, coffee, fruit juice) and a biscuit/cookie.

If you're expecting a large number of guests, it's a good idea to prepare a seating plan like the one opposite.

Then, as each group member arrives, a welcomer assigns him or her to a table and adds the person's name to the plan. This ensures that guests are divided equally between the tables.

Numbering the tables "restaurant-style" will help group members to find their allocated table easily.

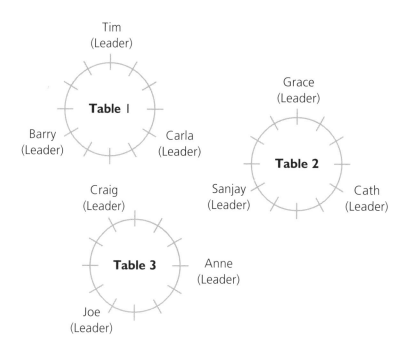

Tim
(Leader)

Table 1

Grace
(Leader)

Barry
(Leader)

Carla
(Leader)

Table 2

Craig
(Leader)

Sanjay
(Leader)

Cath
(Leader)

Table 3

Anne
(Leader)

Joe
(Leader)

📝 *List the people you will ask to be welcomers.*

CATERING

Sharing a meal together is a core component of *Christianity Explored*. It's an opportunity to socialize informally and, for many guests, it may be the only time during the week when someone takes a genuine, personal interest in their lives. Depending on where and when you meet, a meal may not always be possible. But do include it if you can – the benefits in building relationships with group members are well worth the time and effort involved.

Organize a team of people who are willing and able to prepare and serve a meal – this will leave the leaders free to spend time with the group members. This can be an opportunity for church members to be involved with the course without needing to be leaders. If necessary, you can ask guests for a small contribution to help cover the cost.

Resist the temptation to make the food over-elaborate. Keep it simple to eat and clear away. Although it's always good to make an effort, there is a danger that food can end up squeezing out time for exploring the gospel.

⚙ *List the people you will ask to help with the catering.*

PRAYING

Enlisting people to pray regularly for the course is a wonderful way of involving more people in *Christianity Explored*.

- Pray for the preparation of the talks – that they would be faithful to God's word, passionate, challenging and clear.

- Pray for the leaders – that they would be well prepared and that they would "watch [their] life and doctrine closely" (1 Timothy 4:16).

- Pray for the guests – that many would attend; that by his Spirit, God would open their eyes to see who Jesus is, and by his Spirit give them the desire to turn and follow him.

Report back to your prayer team on a weekly basis so that they can pray for specific needs and be encouraged by answered prayer.

⚙ *List the people you will ask to commit themselves to pray for the course.*

Inviting people to come

Although some people will immediately respond positively to an invitation to attend *Christianity Explored*, others will be more reluctant. It's more than likely that they'll be thinking one of three thoughts:

- Christians are weird
  I don't have anything in common with them.

- Christianity is irrelevant
  It's of no practical use to my life.

- Christianity is untrue
  Why should there be only one way to heaven, and why should it have anything to do with Jesus?

Overcoming these objections is a gradual process, and it may be years before some people agree to join a course. Inviting people to events is a great way of helping them to overcome their objections.

VENUE-BASED EVENTS

These events are for people who think that Christians are weird. People who think like this are unlikely to come anywhere near a church.

Venue-based events get around this by enabling people to meet credible Christians outside the church environment.

Think of events you could run in your local area that would appeal to non-Christians (dance lessons, a trip to a place with historic significance, a football game, a visit to an art gallery, a barbecue, etc.).

At such an event, there could be a short Christian talk or testimony, and an invitation to come to *Christianity Explored* to find out more – not an invitation to make a commitment to Jesus Christ.

TOPIC-BASED EVENTS

These events are for people who think that Christianity is irrelevant. People who think like this are unaware that the Bible is God speaking today.

Topic-based events get around this by enabling people to hear talks that address contemporary issues from a Christian perspective.

Think of speakers you could ask to present talks on issues that are important to those you're trying to reach (parenting, stress, terrorism, genetics, fashion, ambition, etc.).

Again, at such an event, there should be an invitation to come to *Christianity Explored* to find out more.

CHURCH-BASED EVENTS

These events are for people who think that Christianity is untrue. People who think like this are unlikely to have heard the gospel preached in years, if at all.

Church-based events get around this by enabling people to attend a church service where the gospel is clearly presented.

Think of ways in which you could specifically tailor a service for such a person (choose hymns with familiar melodies, avoid using Christian "jargon" without carefully explaining it first, make sure the church is warm and welcoming, include testimonies from people who have attended the course, etc.).

Again, at such an event, there should be an invitation to come to *Christianity Explored* to find out more.

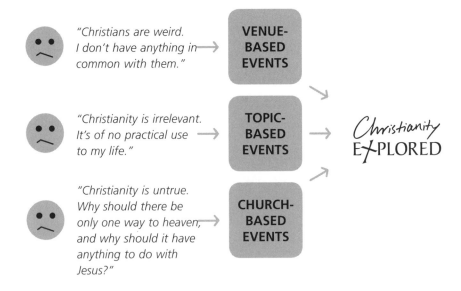

TIPS ON RUNNING EVENTS

- Schedule your events to take place about two weeks before the course begins. Make sure that your church members know about the events in advance, are praying for them, and inviting people to them.

- Get your church involved in planning events. What are your church members passionate about? Could they base an event around that subject?

- Make sure your church members understand the content and reasoning behind the course so that they'll have confidence to invite their friends to events.

- When inviting people to events or to *Christianity Explored*, it is important to be honest about exactly what will happen and who will be there.

- Make "contact cards" and pens available during events so that people can write down their contact details if they're interested in coming to a course. Phone them the week before and remind them that the course is about to begin.

- If an event doesn't go well, celebrate the fact that people have tried.

OTHER WAYS TO INVITE PEOPLE TO THE COURSE

You might want to leave invitations such as the one below at the entrance of your church. It's also a good idea to make them freely available for church members to use when inviting friends, family or colleagues.

Christianity Explored

You don't need to know anything about the Bible.
You won't be asked to read aloud, pray or sing.
You can ask any question you want.

Every Wednesday evening
Starting 9th October to 11th December
7p.m. to 9p.m.
Church, Street, City

If you'd like to come or want to find out more,
please contact ....

Another way of inviting people is to use a survey like the one on the next page. You could make the surveys available at a church service, or even try the survey on people in the street, telling them: "We're from .... Church, and we're doing a survey of people's beliefs – would you have five minutes to answer a few questions?"

You can download an editable version of this survey or order copies of publicity that can be overprinted from **www.ceministries.org**

List your ideas for events you might run.

1. What do you think is the purpose of life?

☐ There is no purpose ☐ Worshipping and serving a god ☐ Job satisfaction
☐ Sexual fulfilment ☐ Achieving personal goals ☐ Serving other people
☐ Love ☐ Having a good time ☐ Making money
☐ Achieving spiritual goals ☐ Advancement of humanity ☐ Friendship
☐ Saving the environment ☐ Achieving social/political goals ☐ Don't know

2. How important is the spiritual dimension in your life?

☐ Very ☐ Fairly ☐ Unimportant ☐ There isn't one ☐ Don't know

3. What do you think happens when a person dies?

☐ Heaven or hell ☐ Heaven for everyone ☐ Purgatory ☐ Another spiritual plane
☐ Reincarnation ☐ Nothing ☐ Don't know ☐ Other

4. What is your view of the Bible?

☐ No longer relevant ☐ Myth / Fable ☐ Moral code
☐ Unreliable document of historical interest ☐ God's message to people ☐ A good story
☐ Important religious text ☐ Don't know ☐ Other

5. What led you to this conclusion?

☐ Family ☐ Spiritual experience ☐ Education ☐ Religious texts
☐ Media ☐ Own investigation ☐ Experience of life ☐ Friends
☐ Don't know ☐ Other

6. What is your view of Christ?

☐ Didn't exist ☐ Good man ☐ Moral teacher ☐ Political figure
☐ Deluded ☐ Deceiver ☐ God in human form ☐ Mythical figure
☐ Prophet ☐ Don't know ☐ Other

7. What led you to this conclusion?

☐ Family ☐ Spiritual experience ☐ Own investigation ☐ Education
☐ Experience of life ☐ Friends ☐ Religious texts ☐ Media
☐ Don't know ☐ Other

8. If you could ask God one question, and you knew it would be answered, what would it be?

Thank you for taking time to complete this questionnaire.

We're also giving out leaflets containing a short explanation of the Christian faith. Would you like to take one?

☐ Yes ☐ No

We run a course called *Christianity Explored*. You can ask any question you want in a relaxed environment – you won't be asked to pray, sing, read or anything like that, and you won't be pestered if you decide not to come again.

Would you be interested in trying such a course? ☐ Yes ☐ No

If yes, please write your name and a contact number / e-mail below:

1 Why evangelize?

📝 *Write down your answer to this question:*

> **What images come to mind when you hear the word "evangelist"?**

Everyone has an image of what an "evangelist" is like. Some people think of a Bible-bashing, street-preaching fanatic. Others think of a money-grubbing, brainwashing TV personality.

Unfortunately, these popular images of the evangelist have sometimes kept us from obeying the Bible's clear command to evangelize (see, for example, Matthew 28:18-20; Luke 24:47; 1 Corinthians 9:16; 2 Corinthians 5:11; 2 Timothy 4:1-5). And actually, the word "evangelist" comes from a Greek word that simply means "someone who brings good news".

📝 *Now answer these questions:*

> **Which Christian person most strongly influenced your decision to follow Christ?**
>
> **What words describe this person and his or her attitude toward you?**

Look at the answers you've written in the boxes above. There is probably a big difference between the stereotypical image of an evangelist and the actual person who "evangelized" you. Most of us first considered Christ because of Christians who told us the good news in a patient, caring, sincere way. That means we all have what it takes to evangelize.

But what is this good news we must pass on?

God created us to be in relationship with him, enjoying his perfect goodness, wisdom, justice, truth and beauty. But we have not been satisfied with God, and have sought our satisfaction in other things. In fact, we love these things more than we love God (Romans 1:25). This rejection of God is what the Bible calls "sin".

God's perfect love and justice mean that he cannot simply ignore sin, because it is neither loving nor just to do so. Instead, we will be judged (Hebrews 9:27), and God's righteous punishment for sin is death (Romans 6:23) and hell (2 Thessalonians 1:9).

However, *"God so loved the world that he gave his one and only Son, that whoever believes in him shall not perish but have eternal life"* (John 3:16). The good news is that Jesus Christ died on the cross to deal with the just condemnation of God. Jesus – the creator himself in human form (Colossians 1:19-20) – died as our substitute (1 Peter 3:18), taking upon himself the punishment we deserve.

God then raised Jesus from the dead. His resurrection is the conclusive sign that Jesus' sacrificial death on behalf of mankind has been accepted by God the Father (Acts 2:32).

If we turn away from our sin, put our trust in Jesus and seek to obey him, we can once again enjoy the uniquely satisfying relationship with God for which we were created.

We do not deserve this extraordinary rescue, and nothing we do can earn it (Ephesians 2:8-9). All we can do is gratefully accept what God has done for us.

And that's why we must evangelize: we must tell people the good news while there is still time.

In each of these three parables, something that is of great value to someone goes missing – a sheep, a coin, a son. In each case, the lost item represents the lost "sinner".

Each parable illustrates how much the lost matter to the Father. The shepherd goes after the sheep until he finds it (v 4); the woman sweeps the house and searches carefully until she finds the coin (v 8); the father's eyes scan the horizon for his son (v 20). In the same way, God seeks out the lost, sending his Son to pay the ultimate price on their behalf.

Jesus tells us that finding what was lost merits great celebration. So much so that verses 7 and 10 show us that there is rejoicing in heaven on the day that any sinner is reunited with God.

You will never set eyes upon someone who does not matter to God, who does not warrant an all-out search, and for whom the whole of heaven would not rejoice if he or she were to bow down and confess Christ as Lord.

2 God's role in evangelism – and ours

We need to distinguish between God's part in evangelism and our part. It's going to be incredibly frustrating if we try to do God's part – because only the Creator of the universe is able to do that.

👁 **Read 2 Corinthians 4:1–6**

📋 *Answer the following questions from the verses you've just read:*

What is God's part in evangelism?

God is shining in our ♡s
to let other(s) know that
His Glory is seen in Jesus Christ

Why can't people see the truth of the gospel?

Satan blinds
the minds of
unbelievers

What is our part in evangelism?

To serve and
deliver God's message.

How should we do our part in evangelism?

Truthfully, respectfully
not manipulatively

What is God's role in evangelism? God makes "his light shine in our hearts to give us the light of the knowledge of the glory of God in the face of Christ" (2 Corinthians 4:6).

In other words, God enables us to recognize that Jesus is God. God makes it possible – by his Holy Spirit – for a person to see who Jesus is. When Paul is on the Damascus Road, he asks: "Who are you, Lord?" and is told: "I am Jesus" (Acts 9:5). That is the moment of his conversion – when he recognizes for the first time who Jesus actually is.

The beginning of 2 Corinthians 4:6 reminds us that God said: "Let light shine out of darkness". That is a reference to the miracle of creation in Genesis 1:3. This same God, who brought light into the world at creation, now shines light into the hearts of human beings, enabling them to see that Jesus is God. In other words, for people to recognize that Jesus is God, God must perform a miracle.

People do not become Christians just because we share the gospel with them. God must shine his light in people's hearts so that they recognize and respond to the truth of the gospel.

And we know from 2 Corinthians 4:4 that people can't see the truth of the gospel because "the god of this age has blinded the minds of unbelievers".

Here, Paul reminds us that we are in the middle of a supernatural battlefield. The reason so many reject the gospel is that the devil is at work, preventing people from recognizing who Jesus is.

The devil blinds people by making them chase after the things of this world, which are passing away and which cannot save them. Their concerns are confined to the here and now: their popularity, their family, their relationships, their material possessions. They are blind to anything beyond that.

As a result, they can only see Jesus in the here and now, perhaps as a great moral teacher; his eternal significance is completely obscured. And, according to verse 4, Satan is determined to prevent people from seeing "the light of the gospel of the glory of Christ, who is the image of God". Satan does not want people to recognize who Jesus is.

OUR ROLE IN EVANGELISM

What then is our role in evangelism? "We ... preach ... Jesus Christ as Lord".

The word "preach" can evoke negative images, but it derives from a word simply meaning "herald", someone who relates important announcements from the king to his kingdom. Our role is to tell people the gospel and leave the Spirit of God to convict them of its truth.

These verses also reveal the attitude we should adopt as we preach. We are to be like "servants for Jesus' sake" (2 Corinthians 4:5). The word translated "servants" literally means "slaves" in Greek. Paul was determined to present Christ to others without any hint of self-promotion.

We must remember that the only difference between ourselves and an unbeliever is that God, in his mercy, has opened our blind eyes and illuminated our hearts by his Holy Spirit. We should be forever grateful, and so seek to promote Christ, not ourselves.

We must keep preaching Christ as Lord and, remembering that only a miracle from God can open blind eyes, we must keep praying that God will shine his light in the hearts of unbelievers.

2 Corinthians 4:1–6 also helps us to carry out our role in the right way: "we do not use deception, nor do we distort the word of God ... by setting forth the truth plainly we commend ourselves to every man's conscience in the sight of God ... For we do not preach ourselves, but Jesus Christ as Lord."

When we tell people about Christ, we should demonstrate the following qualities:

Integrity – "we do not use deception". We are straight with people; we are genuine and sincere, and we never use any kind of emotional manipulation.

Fidelity – we do not "distort the word of God". We have to tell people the tough bits. If, for example, we don't tell people about sin, about hell, and about the necessity of repentance, then we are distorting God's word. Preaching these hard truths means trusting in the work of the Holy Spirit to draw people to Christ, however "difficult" the message.

Humility – "we do not preach ourselves, but Jesus Christ as Lord". We must draw people to Jesus, not to ourselves. We must remember that some people are very impressionable, and that we want them to make a decision to follow Christ because they are convinced by the truth, and are being led by the Holy Spirit, rather than being manipulated by their admiration of the course leader.

As we use *Christianity Explored* to preach the gospel, we must remember that it is up to God whether somebody becomes a Christian or not. Only he can open blind eyes, so we must trust him for the results. God will do his part, and we must do ours.

3 Being a Christianity Explored leader

So, what will it be like to do our part in *Christianity Explored*?

👁 **Read 2 Timothy, chapters 1–2**

With the joy that comes from seeing the lost rescued, we also see the sobering reality of the task ahead. In 2 Timothy 1:8, Paul beseeches Timothy to join him in "suffering" for the gospel. He wrote this around AD 67, chained and shackled in a Roman prison and aware that he was going to die soon. Many followers of Christ had deserted Paul (2 Timothy 1:15), so his appeal to Timothy was not only to join him in suffering for the gospel, but also to guard it, protect it and pass it on.

2 Timothy 2:3–4 is a good model for us as we lead guests through *Christianity Explored*. These verses describe the dedicated soldier for whom hardship, risk and suffering are a matter of course. The Roman African writer, Tertullian, described a soldier's life like this: "No soldier goes to war equipped with luxuries, nor does he go forth to the battle-line from his bed-chamber, but from light and narrow tents wherein every hardship and roughness and uncomfortableness is to be found."[1]

Being a *Christianity Explored* leader doesn't mean you have to live in a tent for the duration of the course – but it will mean the soldier's life: discipline, responsibility and commitment. We need to be committed in three particular areas:

1. Committed to the Bible

2. Committed to prayer

3. Committed to people

1. COMMITTED TO THE BIBLE

God's word is where the power is. Whatever his personal circumstances, Paul knew that if the word were preached, it would do its work: "I am suffering even to the point of being chained like a criminal. But God's word is not chained" (2 Timothy 2:9).

---

1   Tertullian, *Address to the Martyrs*, Part 3. Taken from *The Epistle of the Gallican Churches Lugdunum and Vienna*. With an appendix containing Tertullian's *Address to Martyrs* (trans. T. Herbert Bindley; London: SPCK, 1900), p. 55.

In 2 Timothy 2:15, Paul exhorts Timothy to devote himself to the study of God's word: "Do your best to present yourself to God as one approved, a workman who does not need to be ashamed and who correctly handles the word of truth."

Because we're convinced of the power of God's word, every group member should be given a Mark's Gospel or Bible of their own at the beginning of the course – and our focus as leaders should consistently be on the Bible, specifically Mark's Gospel.

It is vital that you study Mark for yourself and think about its application in your own life. If the message of Mark doesn't excite you, it won't be exciting for those who attend the course.

2. COMMITTED TO PRAYER

Prayer is essential before, during and after the course. Paul opens his letter to Timothy by saying: "Night and day I constantly remember you in my prayers" (2 Timothy 1:3). We, too, need to be constantly remembering the guests and our fellow leaders in our prayers.

Being dedicated to the Bible and prayer means being single-minded. As 2 Timothy 2:4 says: "No-one serving as a soldier gets involved in civilian affairs – he wants to please his commanding officer". Because the work of evangelism is so important, we must be ruthless in organizing our schedules to that end. The course will have a huge impact on our time.

Again and again, as we seek to make time to lead, to study Mark, to pray and to meet up with group members, the good will be the enemy of the best, and the urgent will be the enemy of the important. We may find temptations or feelings of inadequacy creeping in. Sometimes, leading will be a real struggle: physically, emotionally and spiritually. After all, our enemy Satan hates the work we are doing.

But as Paul's illustration of the soldier makes clear, we must remain dedicated. If people stop attending, we keep praying for them. If they don't seem interested in the discussions, we keep studying and teaching Mark. We must not be discouraged, because we do it all for our "commanding officer", the Lord Jesus Christ.

3. COMMITTED TO PEOPLE

God's plan is for the gospel to be communicated life to life. It is not just a matter of us delivering a series of arguments or ideas, brain to brain. We must be prepared to share our lives with this group, and to love them for the sake of Christ. Paul shows us the way in 1 Thessalonians 2:8:

> *"We loved you so much that we were delighted to share with you not only the gospel of God but our lives as well, because you had become so dear to us."*

It is supremely in our lives that our guests at *Christianity Explored* will be given the answers to their objections that Christians are weird, Christianity is irrelevant, or that it is untrue. We are not the gospel (Jesus is), but our lives should make the teaching about God our Saviour attractive (see Titus 2:10).

And that means that we need to show genuine concern for people's lives, their struggles and their questions – and not dismiss them as irrelevant. It means we need to respect them, even when they disagree with us. It means we need to open up our own lives to their inspection, and talk about our own weaknesses and failures, as well as the ways that Christ has changed us. Such genuine love and honesty are the marks of a true disciple of Christ, and in and of themselves they can be a compelling answer to many of the doubts that people have.

Guard against the *Christianity Explored* course being perceived in your church* as the interest and responsibility only of those who are directly involved. The care of our guests on *Christianity Explored* needs to be a matter for the whole church family. Only a comparatively few will be actually running the course. But everyone should take ownership of the project as they pray, invite friends, keep up to date with how the course is going and are ready to welcome and share the on-going care of the guests. This will help to spread the excitement of evangelism, and will be a great encouragement to the whole church family.

But love is never without cost. It will involve us in the complex and messy lives that people have. We must understand that mission means mess. It may require us to offer someone practical help. We should do this willingly, but wisely and prayer-fully, and in consultation with other Christians. But don't shrink back because of the cost.

* If you are running *Christianity Explored* as part of a college Christian Fellowship or other non-church group, the above still applies. Every Christian in your group should be prayerfully supporting the course, inviting friends, and welcoming guests when the opportunity arises.

Two *Christianity Explored* websites to help you:

www.christianityexplored.org
For non-Christians whether or not they're on a course

www.ceministries.org
For leaders looking for information, downloads and resources

4 Before the course

Before the course starts, there are a number of things you should do:

INVITE PEOPLE!

Ask people to be your guests at events organized by your church during which there will be an invitation by the speaker to attend *Christianity Explored*. (See page 21 for ideas for events.)

Or it may be appropriate to invite people directly to the course. Let them know that they will be able to ask any questions they want and that they will not be asked to pray, sing or read aloud.

When inviting people to events or to *Christianity Explored*, it is important to be honest about exactly what will happen and who will be there.

While some people will respond positively to the first invitation they receive, for others it may take months or even years of working towards that point. Don't be discouraged if people don't respond positively right away.

GET TO KNOW MARK'S GOSPEL, THE HANDBOOK AND THE DVD

Read through Mark at least three times. Familiarize yourself with the Handbook that your group will be using, and the guidance on the answers to questions in the Study Guide section of this Leader's Guide (page 67).

As you prepare, make notes in your copy of the group member's Handbook. You will then be able to use your annotated Handbook to lead your group instead of referring back to this Leader's Guide. You will feel much more confident to lead your group once you've prepared for the Bible studies and discussions.

As your group members read through Mark, you will need to be prepared to answer any questions they come up with that arise from the Bible text. There is a section on page 237 that will help you with this. You will need to study and absorb this.

If you are using the *Christianity Explored* DVD, watch each episode through several times. This will help you to become more familiar with the material, and also enable you to refer back to it during discussion. "Do you remember what was said in the DVD?"

GET TO KNOW YOUR FELLOW LEADERS

It is important that people not only hear the gospel explained clearly, but also see it modelled in the life of believers. You will be praying together, studying together, and teaching groups together, so it's important to get to know each other and pray for each other before you begin. Your unity and love for one another will speak volumes about the truth of the gospel message.

PREPARE YOUR TESTIMONY

> "Always be prepared to give an answer to everyone who asks you to give the reason for the hope that you have. But do this with gentleness and respect..." (1 Peter 3:15).

A testimony is an account of God's work in your life. Everybody who has been born again and who is becoming like Christ has a unique, interesting and powerful testimony, regardless of whether or not it appears spectacular.

At some point during the course, you may feel it appropriate to share your testimony with the group. Often someone will ask you directly how you became a Christian and you will need to have an answer ready.

You may find the guidelines below helpful as you prepare your testimony:

▣ Keep it honest, personal and interesting

Tip: Your first sentence should make people sit up and listen. Anything too general, for example: "Well, I was brought up in a Christian home…" may make people switch off immediately.

▣ Keep it short

Tip: Any more than three minutes may stretch people's patience. They can always ask you questions if they want to know more.

▣ Keep pointing to Christ, not yourself

Tip: Your testimony is a great opportunity to communicate the gospel. Always include what it is that you believe, as well as how you came to believe it. As a general guide, try to explain why you think Jesus is God, how his death affects you personally, and what changes God has made in your life.

Prepare your testimony. (List the main points below.) You might find it useful to share your testimony with other leaders and get their feedback.

Gladly making others glad in God.

PREPARE FOR DIFFICULT QUESTIONS

The course starts by asking the group members to answer this question: "If you could ask God one question, and you knew it would be answered, what would it be?" This will draw out a number of questions that will need careful handling. The appendices, starting on page 231, will help you deal with some of the most common questions that people may ask about Christianity in general, and about Mark's Gospel in particular.

PRAY

▣ that those invited will attend the course.

▣ that God would enable you to prepare well.

▣ for the logistics of organizing the course.

▣ for good relationships with your co-leaders and group members.

▣ that God would equip you to lead faithfully.

▣ that the Holy Spirit would open the blind eyes of those who attend.

▣ *Fill in the table below to help you pray for one another.*

Leader's name	Prayer points
1.	
2.	
3.	

▣ *Take time now to pray through the points above.*

5 During the course

The first two chapters of 1 Thessalonians give us a glimpse of the way in which Paul – and the others with him – preached the gospel. They are a useful guide as we seek to relate the gospel to those who participate in the course.

👁 **Read 1 Thessalonians chapters 1–2**

Our hope as we run the course – which is the same hope Paul had as he preached – is that people will understand their need of rescue and turn to "serve the living and true God" (1 Thessalonians 1:9).

In order for that to happen, each part of the session is important. This chapter uses an evening session as an example. Please adapt it to your own situation if you meet at a different time.

Example of an evening session

6:30 p.m.	**Leaders' prayer meeting**
7:00 p.m.	**Guests arrive for the meal**
7:45 p.m.	**Explore (Bible study)**
8:05 p.m.	**Talk/DVD**
8:30 p.m.	**Discuss**
9:00 p.m.	**End of the evening – "One-to-One"**

Note: All times are approximate. You can make certain sections shorter or longer depending on your circumstances.

6:30 P.M. – LEADERS' PRAYER MEETING

Each week, you and your fellow leaders may arrive having had a difficult time at home or at work. Many leaders find themselves coming under spiritual attack as they seek to serve God faithfully. So it is vital to begin the evening by supporting one another in prayer. It may be helpful to focus on a few Bible verses. It is also crucial to pray for the guests. Pray that the gospel will come to them "not simply with words, but also with power, with the Holy Spirit and with deep conviction" (1 Thessalonians 1:5).

7.00 P.M. – MEAL

Having prayed together as leaders, you are ready to welcome the guests as they begin to arrive for the meal. Make a point of learning their names in Session 1. Being greeted by name by a leader in the second week will mean a great deal to guests.

Paul wrote: "We loved you so much that we were delighted to share with you not only the gospel of God but our lives as well, because you had become so dear to us" (1 Thessalonians 2:8). During the meal, it is important to share our lives with the guests. We want them to meet credible, open, caring Christians.

Try to avoid heavy theological discussions during this time. The intention is to share life, not to be spiritually intense. We want people to be able to relax and, above all, to realize that we are interested in every aspect of their well-being, not just the spiritual. Find out about their hobbies, jobs, families, holidays, culture and interests.

7:45 P.M. – EXPLORE

This discussion has two components.

First, groups discuss any questions arising from the previous week's "Follow up" (this home Bible study involves reading a few chapters from the Bible and answering questions).

Second, groups look together at a passage from the Bible.

See pages 11 – 12 of the group member's Handbook for an example of this.

Since not everyone will have done his or her "Follow up" Bible study every week, it's important not to make anyone feel uncomfortable. If nobody has anything they'd like to discuss, move on to the Bible passage for that session.

As Christians, we are entrusted with the gospel, and that means we must present it clearly. We're not presenting our own personal agendas, and we're not seeking to dupe anyone into becoming a Christian. We want group members to be able to make an informed decision about Christ. "For the appeal we make does not spring from error or impure motives, nor are we trying to trick you. On the contrary, we speak as men approved by God to be entrusted with the gospel" (1 Thessalonians 2:3–4).

During the Explore Bible study you may get replies that approach the answer to a question but are not quite complete. Try to guide your group from these initial answers to a better, more biblical answer.

Have further questions in mind to develop the initial answer, for example: "What did you mean by that?", "What does everyone else think?", "Where does it say that?"

If someone gives a wrong answer, it may be tempting to correct them immediately. Instead, try opening up the discussion by asking others what they think, for example: "Does everyone agree with Jane?"

Don't be afraid to correct a wrong answer graciously if you think the answer will take the group too far "off topic," for example: "Thank you John, that's an interesting point, but I'm not sure that's what's going on here."

Sometimes, individual personalities may make it difficult to conduct an effective group discussion:

- **The silent type** – never contributes to the discussion. She's best helped by encouraging people to work through questions in groups of two or three at points during the study and then having them feed their answers back to the main group.

- **The talkative type** – likes to monopolize the discussion. Depending on how well you know him, either subdivide the group into smaller groups to give others an opportunity to speak, or have a quiet and tactful word with him (for example: "Tim, thanks so much for everything you're contributing. I wonder if you could help me with the quieter members of the group…")

- **The arguer** – attacks the answers given by everyone else in the group. It's best to take him aside at the end of the evening and listen to any specific issues he may have. If the problem persists, it may be appropriate to remove him from the group, asking him to meet with you "one-to-one" at a different time.

- **The know-it-all** – immediately answers every question, thus stifling the group. This situation is best dealt with by supplementary questions to facilitate group discussion (for example: "Does everyone agree with Nick?").

- **The off-on-a-tangent type** – loves to steer the discussion away from the topic and talk about something entirely different. It may be that this new subject is something the whole group wants to explore, but if not, tactfully suggest that it might be good to discuss it more fully at the end of the evening.

8.05 P.M. – LISTEN

At this point in the evening, the course leader presents a talk (or a DVD is shown).

If you've heard the talks – or watched the DVDs – before, it can be tempting to switch off and stop listening, but bear in mind that if you don't listen, guests won't either.

8:30 P.M. – DISCUSS

Start this discussion by asking: "Did anything particularly strike you from the talk?" or "Was there anything that stood out from the talk/DVD?" Then use the printed questions to encourage discussion as you explore together the truths that have been presented.

See page 14 of the group member's Handbook for an example of this.

Having spent a while listening, it's important that guests now feel able to speak freely. Although there will be opportunities to teach, the leader's primary role in this group discussion is therefore to listen and to ensure that everyone is heard. "But we were gentle among you, like a mother caring for her little children" (1 Thessalonians 2:7).

- Leaders should try to avoid speaking immediately after each other.

- You may feel it is appropriate to "carry over" a discussion from the Explore Bible study, if you were unable to adequately cover an important issue.

- Be gracious and courteous, and act as peacemaker if the discussion gets heated.

- If a question is met with silence, don't be too quick to say something. Allow people time to think.

- It may be appropriate in certain circumstances to address a question directly to an individual in order to encourage discussion (for example: "Sam, what do you think about this?")

- If one person's particular issue begins to dominate, gently ask him or her if you can talk about the issue together at the end of the session.

- Don't forget how important the tone of your voice and your body language can be as you seek to further the discussion.

- Lead honestly. You won't be able to deal with all the questions thrown your way, so don't pretend to have all the answers. Some questions can be easily addressed, but others will be difficult. If you don't know the answer, say so – but try to have an answer ready for the following week.

9:00 P.M. – END OF THE EVENING – "ONE-TO-ONE"

The course leader will bring the evening to a formal close and ask guests to complete the "Follow up" in their Handbook before the following week. Invite them to stay a while longer if they'd like to chat things through, but make it clear that they are free to go – as promised – at 9 p.m. This is another small way of earning people's trust.

It is at this point that the most effective conversations take place, because you have time to talk "one-to-one" with guests. "For you know that we dealt with each of you as a father deals with his own children, encouraging, comforting and urging you to live lives worthy of God" (1 Thessalonians 2:11–12).

6:30 p.m.
Leaders' Prayer Meeting

"Pray that the gospel will come to guests "not simply with words, but also with power, with the Holy Spirit and with deep conviction."

1 Thessalonians 1:5

←

7:00 p.m.
Meal

"We loved you so much that we were delighted to share with you not only the gospel of God but our lives as well, because you had become so dear to us."

1 Thessalonians 2:8

←

7:45 p.m. Explore
8:05 p.m. Listen

"For the appeal we make does not spring from error or impure motives, nor are we trying to trick you. On the contrary, we speak as men approved by God to be entrusted with the gospel."

1 Thessalonians 2:3–4

←

8:30 p.m.
Discuss

"But we were gentle among you, like a mother caring for her little children."

1 Thessalonians 2:7

←

9:00 p.m.
"One-to-One"

"For you know that we dealt with each of you as a father deals with his own children, encouraging, comforting and urging you to live lives worthy of God."

1 Thessalonians 2:11-12

←

We do all these things in the hope that guests will turn "to serve the living and true God."
1 Thessalonians 1:9

6 Identity, mission and call in Mark's Gospel

As a leader preparing to teach Mark, there's no substitute for reading through his Gospel at least two or three times.

And as you read, you'll begin to see three great themes in Mark:

■ Who is Jesus? (Jesus' identity)

■ Why did he come? (Jesus' mission)

■ What does it mean to follow him? (Jesus' call)

And the backdrop which creates such drama in Mark is his interest in people's spiritual *blindness* to these issues.

IDENTITY

Mark 8 is the chapter on which the book hinges. Beginning in Mark 8:27 we find all three of these themes – identity, mission and call – in quick succession. Before that, Mark sets the scene in Mark 8:22-26 with the unusual healing of a blind man. In the healing process the blind man moves from seeing *nothing* to seeing *something*, then to seeing *everything*.

It seems that Mark records the miracle here to help his readers see that the disciples are going through a similar process as their spiritual blindness is being overcome.

Let's take a few verses at a time.

👁 **Read Mark 8:27–30**

The dominant question in verses 27–30 is Jesus' *identity*. Who exactly is Jesus?

People had lots of theories, just as they do now: "Some say John the Baptist; others say Elijah; and still others, one of the prophets" (Mark 8:28). They put Jesus in the category of a man sent from God. But actually they are still blind to his true identity. He is not another prophet. He is the one to whom all the prophets pointed.

But Jesus gets very personal in verse 29: "What about you? ... Who do you say I am?"

This is like a mid-term examination for the disciples. There had been lots of debate about the identity of Jesus, and they had seen plenty of evidence pointing to the answer Peter gives here, that Jesus is God's chosen and promised King.

The book of Isaiah talks about the coming of the Christ, God's only chosen King:

> "Be strong, do not fear; your God will come, he will come with vengeance; with divine retribution he will come to save you.
>
> Then will the eyes of the blind be opened and the ears of the deaf unstopped. Then will the lame leap like a deer, and the mute tongue shout for joy" (Isaiah 35:4-6).

Through the prophet Isaiah, God told his people how they would recognize the Christ, his promised King, when he came: the deaf will hear, the blind will see, the lame will walk, and the mute will speak. Among many other miracles recorded in the first half of Mark's Gospel, Jesus makes a lame man walk in chapter 2, he makes a deaf and mute man hear and speak in chapter 7, and he cures a blind man in chapter 8. Jesus demonstrates his power in this specific way so that people will recognize him as the Christ.

👁 Read Mark 1:2–3

The second half of the quotation (verse 3) is from Isaiah 40 – a passage that makes it clear that this "Lord" who is mentioned is the creator of the world, the one who miraculously delivered his people from Egypt. Mark tells us that John the Baptist is the "voice of one calling in the desert" who will prepare the way for the Lord. When John baptizes Jesus, the voice from heaven confirms that Jesus is indeed the unique Son of God, the promised Lord of Isaiah 40 (Mark 1:11).

However, despite seeing and hearing Jesus in action, there was much discussion, (see Mark 1:27; 2:7, 10-12, 23-28; 4:41; 5:35-42; 6:1-3; 8:14-21). It might seem as if the disciples were never going to get the issue of Jesus' identity right. But Mark inserts the healing of the blind man to signal to us that a miracle is taking place. The disciple's spiritually blind eyes are being opened to see the true identity of Jesus. Peter answers the question concerning Jesus' identity correctly: "You are the Christ". But is Peter now seeing everything clearly?

MISSION

So far in Mark we have been given clear indications of the *mission* of Jesus. For example, he gave priority to preaching over healing (Mark 1:35-39), and to spiritual health over physical health (Mark 2:5). His choice of company raised questions,

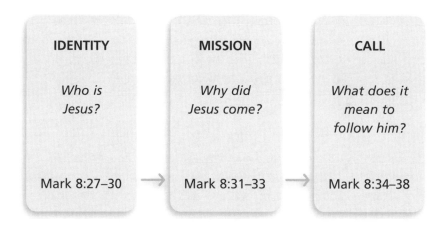

IDENTITY	MISSION	CALL
Who is Jesus?	*Why did Jesus come?*	*What does it mean to follow him?*
Mark 8:27–30	Mark 8:31–33	Mark 8:34–38

but Jesus shows that this is deliberate policy (Mark 2:15-17). This is his mission, to preach the good news, and call sinners. But how can sinners be accepted by God?

👁 **Read Mark 8:31–33**

Here, for the first time, Jesus begins to teach that he "must suffer many things and be rejected by the elders, chief priests and teachers of the law, and that he must be killed and after three days rise again". This is why he has come.

Jesus leaves no room for misunderstanding – he speaks "plainly about this" (verse 32) – because this is his mission and he knows that the disciples, and most of the public, have a very different idea of what the Christ will be like. Their idea is of a triumphant king, marching in to claim his territory, trampling the enemy underfoot, and ushering in a glorious new era for his followers. A Christ who was going to suffer and die would have seemed like a contradiction in terms.

In chapter 8, although Peter has Jesus' *identity* right, it's clear he hasn't yet understood Jesus' *mission*. He has this triumphal view of the Christ in mind when he takes Jesus aside and begins "to rebuke him" (Mark 8:32). But Jesus' strong reaction shows just how necessary death is to his mission: "Get behind me, Satan! ... You do not have in mind the things of God, but the things of men" (Mark 8:33).

Jesus clearly knew that Peter's failure to understand his mission was a result of Satan blinding Peter to it. The idea that the Son of God had to suffer and die is still a stumbling block for many people today. But if we're to understand correctly Mark's Gospel – and indeed the whole Bible – it is essential to grasp the true nature of Jesus' mission: he "must suffer" and "he must be killed" (Mark 8:31) so that we can be forgiven. And we must see that this is one of the "things of God" that Peter did not have in mind.

Jesus re-affirmed the nature of his mission in 9:30-32; 10:32-34, 45; 12:1-12 and 14:27-28. Like the disciples, many people struggle to hold the identity and mission of Jesus in tension. How can he be the Son of God, and also the man who hung dead on a cross? But this is the power of the gospel message.

CALL

It is fascinating to see the absolute authority Jesus has as he calls people to follow him (see Mark 1:16-20; 2:13-14). The New Testament explains that as we teach the truth about Jesus, God opens blind eyes and calls people to him. And they come as they are. They come, even though it means leaving the life they had made for themselves. They come, because they now see that Jesus, and the salvation he offers, is the ultimate treasure.

👁 Read Mark 8:34–38

Jesus is very candid about the implications of being his follower. Having just spoken to the disciples about his own death, Jesus calls the crowd to him and says: "If anyone would come after me, he must deny himself and take up his cross and follow me". It is striking to see Jesus immediately turn his attention from the cross *he* must take up, to the cross *we* must take up.

If we are to follow him, Jesus tells us we must deny ourselves. It is not a natural thing for human beings to turn away from self-centeredness and self-reliance, but that is Jesus' call. Following him means giving the throne of our lives to him.

And we cannot follow Jesus if we do not take up our cross. The cross was the ultimate sign of humanity's rejection of Jesus. (See Mark 12:1-12, especially verses 7 and 10). Jesus makes it plain that those who follow him will face rejection in this world, where he is still disowned.

Why would anyone be willing to deny themselves, and take up their cross, as they follow Jesus? The answer is that belonging to him is the only way to be saved. If that seems irrational, we need to hear what Jesus says next:

> "For whoever wants to save his life will lose it, but whoever loses his life for me and for the gospel will save it" (Mark 8:35).

It sounds like the complete opposite of what we would instinctively think. We would naturally prefer to stay in control of our lives, and to avoid the rejection of friends, family and colleagues that comes from being Jesus' followers. But that will mean we walk away from Jesus – the only one who is able to save us.

Just in case we think that following Jesus sounds like a bad deal, verses 35–38 of chapter 8 give us four very good reasons to follow him:

- If we give up our life for him, we'll save it; and if we don't, we'll lose it (8:35).

- If, by rejecting Jesus, we gain the whole world, we still lose the most important thing we have (8:36).

- If we miss out on eternal life, there's nothing we can do to buy it back (8:37).

- If we reject Jesus, then he will reject us when he returns as Judge of the world (8:38).

This will be a tough world to live in as a follower of Christ. Jesus does not downplay that reality. And as we share the good news with people, we must be prepared to tell them what it means to follow Jesus now. But if they have heard his call, they will come, even though it means substantial changes in their lives. They will come, because they now see that Jesus – and the salvation he offers – is the ultimate treasure.

Yet the evidence shows us that the disciples were still at least partly blind to the call of Jesus to deny themselves. After he explained about his mission again in Mark 9:30-32, we discover in 9:33-34 that the disciples responded by arguing among themselves about which of them was the greatest. Then, in spite of Jesus' clear correction in 9:35-37 and again in 10:13-14, we find James and John wanting to share glory with Jesus in 10:35-37.

They were still struggling to see the implications of the call of Jesus on their lives. Peter famously denied knowing Jesus, rather than denying himself, for fear of the implications of being his disciple.

Yet the Lord Jesus graciously and patiently worked with them during his years of public ministry, before and after his death and resurrection. The journey of the disciples to properly seeing who Jesus is, why he came and what it means to follow him is the journey that many course members are on. This makes Mark's Gospel a great book for evangelism.

Understanding the identity, mission and call of Jesus is the core of Mark's message, and the basis of salvation. Talking to course members about these three great themes in Mark, and asking them who they think Jesus is, why he came and what it means to follow him, is a great way to work out where they are spiritually, and how we can help them move forward.

THE IMPORTANCE OF IDENTITY, MISSION, CALL

A guest's understanding of Jesus' identity, mission and call is crucial to the way in which he or she will respond to the gospel message.

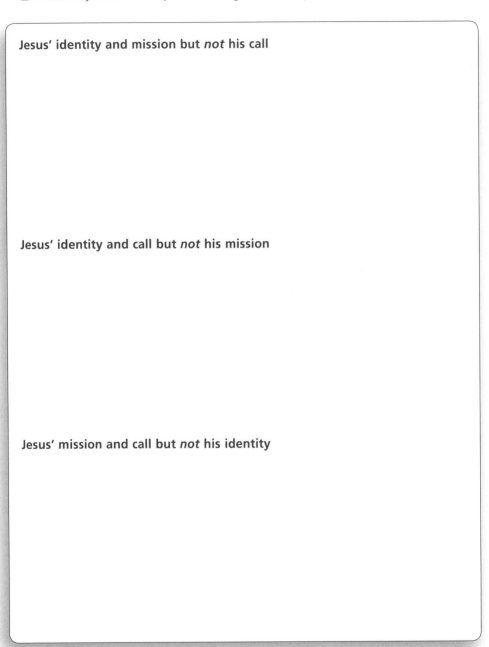 *What do you think the problems might be for a person who has understood:*

Jesus' identity and mission but *not* his call

Jesus' identity and call but *not* his mission

Jesus' mission and call but *not* his identity

There are a number of implications that arise in each instance. For example:

If a person understands Jesus' identity and mission, but not his call, they won't understand the need to deny themselves or take up their cross. As a result, their lives won't be changed and, because any suffering they face will be unexpected, they are likely to become disillusioned and turn away from Christianity.

If a person understands Jesus' identity and call, but not his mission, they won't understand the seriousness of their sin or the fact that Jesus has paid the price for it. As a result, they won't know the joy of forgiveness. Because they have not understood what grace means, their life will become a dutiful and "religious" dirge. They will either become self-righteous or become paralyzed by their sense of failure. Because they have not understood the cross, they can have no assurance of eternal life with God. Failure to understand the seriousness of sin is likely to leave them hugely discouraged by the evil they see in the world.

If a person understands Jesus' mission and call, but not his identity, they won't understand that Jesus is God. As a result, they will see Jesus merely as an example of how one might live. There will be no consistent motivation to live the Christian life. They won't know that God loves them or that God is sovereign over their life.

🔁 *Think about how you became a Christian and answer the following:*

When did you first understand who Jesus is?
Who helped you to see his identity?

When did you understand why Jesus came?
Was it a person, an event or something else that first helped you understand his mission?

At what point did you realize what Jesus demands of you?
Was this clear to you at once, or was it a gradual process?

📷 *Look through Mark's Gospel and decide what each paragraph has to say about Jesus' identity, mission or call. Label each one "I," "M" or "C," remembering that some paragraphs may be a combination of two or three of the above.*

7 After the course

Christianity Explored is not a seven-session conveyor belt that either ships unbelievers into the Christian faith – or tips them off into the street outside. It is therefore vital to have a coherent follow-up strategy in place for all guests.

GIVE OUT FEEDBACK FORMS

Feedback forms, given out during the last session of the course, are a great way to challenge course members to think about where they currently are with Christ, and to help leaders plan a way forward once the course is ended.

You can find a sample feedback form on page 58. An editable version of this form can be downloaded from **www.ceministries.org**

STAY IN TOUCH

Having spent seven sessions with your group considering profound and personal issues, you will know them well – and they will know you well.

Under these circumstances, it would clearly be wrong to "drop" group members once the course comes to an end. Whatever their response has been, God has not given up on them, and neither should you.

Furthermore, if the friends who invited these people along see leaders maintaining a genuine interest in the guests, they will feel more confident about bringing others along in future.

Plan to stay in touch with all the members of your group, and arrange it with your co-leaders so that each group member has at least one Christian who remains in touch with him or her.

Feedback Form

You don't have to answer all the questions if you don't want to, but please be as honest as you can.

Your details (optional):

Name _____   Date _____

Address _____

Telephone _____   Email _____

1. Before you began *Christianity Explored*, how would you have described yourself?

☐ I didn't believe in God

☐ I wasn't sure if God existed or not

☐ I believed in God but not in Jesus Christ

☐ A Christian (that is, personally committed to Jesus Christ)

☐ Something else _____

2. How would you describe yourself now in relation to Jesus Christ?

☐ I understand who Jesus is, why he came and what it means to follow him. I have put my trust in him.

☐ I am interested in learning more but, as yet, I have not put my trust in Jesus.

☐ Other _____

3. If you have not yet put your trust in Jesus, what is stopping you?

4. Do you know for certain that you have eternal life?

☐ Yes   ☐ No

5. Suppose you were to die tonight and God asked: "Why should I let you into heaven?" What would you say?

6. What would you like to do now?

☐ I would like to join *Discipleship Explored* (a course that will help me to continue in the Christian life).

☐ I would like to come to *Christianity Explored* again.

☐ I would like a copy of the *Christianity Explored* book in order to review what I've learned.

☐ I do not wish to do anything further at this stage.

☐ I would like to join a church.

☐ I am happy at the church I go to, which is _____

7. Would you like to make any comments about the course, either positive or negative?

ARRANGE FOLLOW-UP FOR NEW BELIEVERS

If anyone in your group has made a commitment to Christ, it's vital to help them lay firm foundations so that they will be able to persevere.

Discipleship Explored, based on the book of Philippians, is one way of doing this. The *Discipleship Explored* course has a similar format to *Christianity Explored* and lasts for eight sessions. An alternative would be to use the Universal edition, which is a Bible study that uses clear and simple English to make it as widely accessible as possible. You can find out more about both versions of *Discipleship Explored* at **www.ceministries.org**

You should also invite new believers to start coming along to church with you if they're not already regularly attending. It is often a difficult task to get people into the habit of meeting together regularly on a Sunday, but the concept of a Christian who doesn't belong to a church is foreign to the New Testament, so help them to take this seriously (Hebrews 10:25). Introduce them to other Christians and help them to become integrated within the church by joining a Bible-study group and finding an area of service within which they can participate.

ARRANGE FOLLOW-UP FOR THOSE WHO HAVEN'T YET MADE A COMMITMENT

Ask whether they are interested in exploring Christianity further. If they are, one option is to invite them to come back and go through *Christianity Explored* again – some people have gone through the course three or more times before they felt ready to make a commitment. Remember that they aren't just re-hearing the talks but re-reading Mark's Gospel as well, which will work on their hearts each time it is opened.

RECOMMEND OR GIVE AWAY BOOKS

Reading a good Christian book at the right time can be very influential. Think carefully about the books you have read and see if any of them would suit particular members of your group. If you're not an avid reader, ask around for advice about books suitable for people in different situations.[2]

---

2   Two paperbacks accompany the *Christianity Explored* course: "One life. What's it all about?" and "If you could ask God one question…". You could also look at the "Go Deeper" sections in the Tough Questions area of the *Christianity Explored* website (choose a question from www. christianityexplored.org/tough-questions, and then click on the "Go Deeper" bar).

READ THE BIBLE WITH A GROUP MEMBER

You might suggest getting together with an individual on a regular basis to read through a book of the Bible. This can be totally informal; just two friends with an open Bible finding out what God's word has to say to them.

Questions to guide your study could be:

What does the passage mean?

◾ Are there any difficult words or ideas that merit special attention?

What does the passage mean in context?

◾ What comes before/after the passage?

◾ Why is the passage placed where it is?

◾ Is it addressed to a specific individual or group of people? Why?

What does the passage mean for us?

◾ What have we learned about ourselves?

◾ About God?

◾ How do we apply the passage to our lives?

PRAY

A supremely Christ-like way of caring for people is to pray for them. Even after the course has ended, it is important to pray for all the members of the group.

For new believers, pray for growth, fruitfulness and joy.

For those who have not yet made a commitment, pray that the Lord will have mercy on them and send his Holy Spirit to open their blind eyes.

Pray for yourself, for patience and wisdom as you wait for God's word to do its work.

📧 *After the course has ended, use this space to write down the names of those in your care, and the ways in which you will aim to support them.*

SUGGESTIONS FOR NEXT TIME

If you are the course leader, it's very helpful to find out what you're doing right, and perhaps ways in which you might improve future courses. In addition to the feedback forms from guests, ask the leaders to tell you their thoughts about the course. The following form is one way to do that – or you could meet together after the course to discuss these questions. An editable version of this form can be downloaded from **www.ceministries.org**

Example feedback form for leaders

We are always looking to improve *Christianity Explored* and would value your feedback. The training and support of leaders is an essential part of the course and your comments would be very much appreciated. Please be as honest as possible.

1. What encouraged you most about leading?

2. What did you find most difficult about leading?

3. What did you think of the leaders' training prior to the course?

4. Could we have prepared you better for the course? If so, how?

5. What did you think of the leaders' prayer meetings?

6. What did you think of the course material?

7. Do you have any comments to make about the day away? How could it be improved?

8. Please feel free to comment on any other aspects of the course.

8 Getting our expectations right

Jesus was the most brilliant teacher who ever lived. Nevertheless, a glance through Mark chapter 3 reminds us that:

- Those in authority wanted him dead (v 6).

- The public were often more interested in his miracles than in his teaching (v 9–10).

- One of his own followers would eventually betray him (v 19).

- His own family thought he was out of his mind (v 21).

- Many religious people thought he was evil (v 22).

Yet, in spite of all this pressure, rather than change his approach or water down his message, Jesus continued to teach: "With many similar parables Jesus spoke the word to them, as much as they could understand" (Mark 4:33).

We, too, will face pressure. So why should we persist in teaching God's word to people who don't seem to be listening, or who openly oppose us?

Jesus gives us the answer in Mark chapter 4: God's word produces dramatic results (v 8, 20, 32). But he begins by warning us to expect disappointment and delay.

EXPECT DISAPPOINTMENT

👁 Read Mark 4:1–8, 14–20

The seed (which is "the word," as Jesus explains in v 14) can fall in unfruitful places:

- along the path (v 15)

- on rocky places (v 16)

- among thorns (v 18)

There will be those who delight us by turning up for the first session, but who never come again. There will be those who joyfully make a commitment in Session 7 but, because of family pressure, they soon decide it's just not worth the trouble. Then there are those who diligently attend each week of the course but decide right at the end that their material possessions mean more to them than anything they've heard.

It can be desperately disappointing to see group members apparently respond to the gospel message, but then show no sign of lasting change. But Jesus warns us to expect it.

EXPECT DELAY

👁 **Read Mark 4:26–29**

Jesus uses the metaphor of the seed with good reason: it takes time for seed to grow.

The farmer has to be patient: "Night and day, whether he sleeps or gets up, the seed sprouts and grows, though he does not know how" (Mark 4:27). He just has to trust that the seed will grow, even though it may seem that nothing much is happening.

We live in an instant culture – instant food, instant information, instant credit – and we may find ourselves expecting guests to acquire an instant relationship with God. But delay is as much a part of our work as it is the farmer's. We must be prepared to stay in touch with group members for weeks, months, or even years after the course ends.

There will be those who seem to agree with everything they learn through the course. You decide to meet up with them on a regular basis and, a year later, they still agree with everything they've learned. But they're not Christians.

There may be times when we lose patience and are tempted to give up. But we must continue to plant the word in people's lives, trusting in its power, and remembering that God's timescale is very different from our own.

EXPECT DRAMATIC RESULTS

👁 **Read Mark 4:30–32**

Despite the inevitable disappointments and delays, there is a good reason to continue sowing God's word in people's lives, just as Jesus did: "when planted, it grows and becomes the largest of all garden plants, with such big branches that the birds of the air can perch in its shade" (Mark 4:32). Even a tiny seed – like the mustard seed – can produce dramatic results.

There will be those who bring up the same difficult issues week after week. Then suddenly one of those people will arrive one week and tell you he or she has become a Christian. A year later that person is a *Christianity Explored* leader, and a few months after that, that same person is taking every opportunity to grow in their own understanding in order to be able to teach the gospel more clearly to others.

As Jesus tells us in Mark 4:20, there will be those who hear the word, accept it, and then go on to "produce a crop – thirty, sixty or even a hundred times what was sown".

It is a great encouragement to remember that the power to change lives is not in our eloquence – it is in God's word. So, whatever disappointments we suffer, whatever delays we endure, and whatever circumstances we face, we must continue to preach the word faithfully.

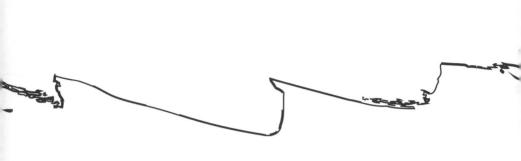

Study Guide

Two *Christianity Explored* websites to help you:

www.christianityexplored.org
This website is for non-Christians, whether or not they are on a course. It features a visual gospel outline based on the Gospel of Mark, answers to common questions, and testimonies from a wide variety of people, as well as information about the *Christianity Explored* course. You can find more details at the back of this book, on page 255.

www.ceministries.org
For leaders looking for information, downloads and resources.

Introduction

This Study Guide section contains talk outlines and studies to work through over the seven-session course. It includes all the material in the group member's Handbook. However it also contains specific instructions for leaders, additional notes and the answers to each question.

- Don't worry if you don't have time to go through all of the questions with your group – the most important thing is to listen to the guests and answer their questions.

- Try to avoid using "jargon" that might alienate group members. Bear in mind that words and phrases familiar to Christians (for example, "pagan," "washed in the blood," "house group," "the Lord" and so on) may seem strange to those outside Christian circles.

- If guests miss a week, take time during the meal to summarize briefly what was taught the week before.

- Some guests may believe that the Bible is not reliable as a source of history. If this issue arises during a group discussion, refer them to the section on the reliability of Mark's Gospel on page 62 of their Handbook.

GOOD NEWS
What are we doing here?

1

- *Welcome the guests to* Christianity Explored *and introduce yourself. Make sure everyone has been introduced to each other. Try to remember names ready for next week.*

- *Give a brief introduction. If you have more than one discussion group, this is best given by the course leader or speaker to everyone together. (The wording below is intended only as a general guide.)*

As we begin, I want to reassure you that:

- You won't be asked to read aloud, pray, sing or do anything that makes you feel uncomfortable.

- We aren't going to take your phone number and pester you. If you decide not to come back, we are still delighted you made time to come today.

- You can ask any question you want, or alternatively feel free just to sit and listen.

Over the next seven sessions we will explore three questions that cut right to the heart of Christianity: Who was Jesus? Why did he come? What is involved in following him?

We also want to spend time addressing whatever questions are important to you. As well as having times of discussion in groups, we will be available to chat at the end of the evening.

We want to give you the opportunity to encounter the real Jesus. That's why we are going to work our way through one book of the Bible, Mark's Gospel.

We want you to be able to check out the facts for yourself. That's why we will give you a reading plan that will take you right through Mark in manageable sections, so that you can examine the evidence for yourself.

Please feel free to make notes and list questions you may have as you listen to the Bible talk. There is space for notes in your Handbook.

◉ *Give each guest a Mark's Gospel or Bible and a Handbook.*

◉ *Ask the group to turn to Session 1 on page 5 of the Handbook.*

◉ *Explain the four sections of the Handbook:*

> **Explore** = we read the Bible together and talk about what we've read (different in Week 1).
>
> **Listen** = we listen to the Bible talk, or watch the DVD, and make notes in the talk outline in the Handbook.
>
> **Discuss** = we discuss some of the points from the Bible talk.
>
> **Follow up** = you read some of Mark for yourself, then bring any questions you have to the group.

Show the guests how to find Mark in their Bibles (if you're using full Bibles) and the verse and chapter divisions, eg: Mark 1:1 – 3:6. You may want to explain that Mark didn't divide his book into chapters and verses. These were added later to help us find our way around.

EXPLORE

◉ *Ask your group the following questions. The first two are not in the Handbook.*

What's your name and what made you come on *Christianity Explored*?

This question is designed to help the group members get to know each other, and to help you begin to understand why they have come on the course.

What is the best news you have ever heard?

This question acts as an icebreaker, and also introduces the subject of "good news" before the talk/DVD.

◉ *Ask your group to turn to the question on page 5 of the Handbook.*

If you could ask God one question, and you knew it would be answered, what would it be?

Ask your group to share their answers if they're happy to do so. Note down what they are so that you can deal with them at some point during the course. Do listen carefully to every question and assure your group that there will be an opportunity to return to them during *Christianity Explored*. (Some questions will be answered by the Bible studies and talks/DVDs and some – like questions about suffering – are best dealt with after the talks about sin or the cross.) *See page 245 for guidance on common questions.*

As a supplementary question, ask your group:

Think about the god you are asking that question to. What is that god like?

This will help you to get a feel for people's current views of God. You may want to refer back to some of these views later on in the course as the character of God becomes clear through his Son, Jesus.

LISTEN

- *(Page 6 in the group member's Handbook) Encourage the group to make notes and list questions they may have as they listen to the Bible talk or watch the DVD. There is space in the Handbook to make notes.*

- *Note: Christianity Explored is based on the 1984 version of the New International Version (NIV). If you are using the 2011 revised NIV, you will find that "Jesus Christ" in Mark 1:1 has been changed to "Jesus the Messiah". The change from "Christ" to "Messiah" does not change the meaning of the verse, since the terms mean the same. They speak of the King who God promised to send into the world. "Christ" is from the Greek word, "Messiah" comes from the Hebrew.*

"The beginning of the gospel about Jesus Christ..." Mark 1:1

- When we look at the natural beauty of the world, and the design of the human body, the question is: Did this all happen by chance? Or did someone create it?

- The Bible says God is the one who created the universe we live in and the bodies we inhabit. So how can we know him?

- We can know God by looking at Jesus Christ.

- Christianity is about Christ – a title that means "God's only chosen King".

- Christianity is the "gospel" – the good news – about Jesus Christ.

- When Jesus was baptized, God the Father announced: "You are my Son".

- God has revealed himself in human history through Jesus Christ. When we look at Jesus, all the guessing games about God stop.

DISCUSS

(Page 7 in the group member's Handbook) Ask your group if there was anything that stood out or particularly struck them from the talk/DVD. This will help them to respond specifically to what they have just heard, before moving on to the group discussion questions.

Is there anything that intrigues or puzzles you about Jesus?

The answers to this question will help you to get a feel for the members of your group and their current thoughts about Jesus. Don't feel that you need to comment on everything they say – there will be plenty of time during the course to address any wrong ideas. However, if you know that something will be looked at in a future session, do let the group members know that you will be discussing it at that point.

How do you feel about reading Mark's Gospel?

Have the group members understood from the talk that Christianity is about Jesus Christ, and that Mark tells us the "good news" about Jesus? This means that reading Mark's Gospel is a great way to explore Christianity.

Some of your group may be unsure or worried about reading through a whole book of the Bible. Reassure them that you will help them with any questions they have about what they've read.

FOLLOW UP

▣ *(Page 8 in the group member's Handbook) Let the group know what section of Mark you would like them to read for this week's Follow Up, and check that they know how to find it in their Mark's Gospel or Bible.*

▣ *Show the group how to approach their personal reading plan by doing question 1 with them. This will reassure any who are nervous about studying the Bible in this way – and will also reduce the amount of home study they need to do for this first week.*

👁 **Read Mark 1:1-20**

> **1. The word "gospel" means "good news". Mark begins his book of good news with three statements about Jesus.**
>
> **a) by the Old Testament prophets (messengers) (Mark 1:2-3)**
>
> **b) by John the Baptist (Mark 1:7)**
>
> **c) by God himself (Mark 1:11)**
>
> **What do they each say about Jesus?**

a) The Old Testament prophets pointed to Jesus as the Lord. They said someone would come before him to prepare the way for him.

b) John the Baptist, himself a great prophet, said that Jesus is "more powerful" than him.

c) God describes Jesus as his own Son, whom he loves and with whom he is pleased.

👁 **Read Mark 1:21 – 2:17**

> **2. In chapters 1 and 2 Jesus shows his authority in different situations. (See Mark 1:16–20, 21–22, 23–28, 40–45; 2:1–12.)**
> **When Jesus speaks or acts, what sorts of things happen?**

▣ He calls people, who immediately drop what they are doing and follow him (Mark 1:16-20).

▣ People are astonished because he teaches with authority, and not like their religious leaders (Mark 1:21-22).

75

- He rebukes evil spirits, and they leave (Mark 1:23-28).

- He heals sickness, even the most serious illnesses (Mark 1:29-34, 40-45).

- He forgives sins (Mark 2:1-12).

- *Note: Christianity Explored is based on the 1984 version of the New International Version (NIV). If you are using the 2011 revised NIV, you will find that "Filled with compassion" in Mark 1:41 has been changed to "Jesus was indignant". If "indignant" is a better translation, it does not diminish the compassion Jesus felt for the man. He was indignant at the man's suffering, and expressed his compassion by confirming his willingness to touch and heal the man.*

👁 Read Mark 2:18 – 3:6

> **3. Even at this early stage, Jesus divided opinions. Some people were amazed by him, while others were enraged.**
> **What are your early impressions of Jesus?**

Mark's design in writing the first part of his Gospel is to prompt the question: "Who is Jesus?" Question 3 is designed to encourage group members to reflect on what they have learned about the identity of Jesus.

> **Do you have any questions about Mark 1:1 – 3:6?**

The next session will start with group members being asked if they have any questions about the section of Mark they read at home. You will find help in answering difficult questions from Mark's Gospel in the appendix on page 237.

IDENTITY
Who is Jesus?

EXPLORE

▪ Ask the guests to turn to Session 2 on page 11 of the Handbook.

▪ Ask if they have any questions from last session's Follow up. The appendix on page 237 lists common questions from Mark along with suggestions for answering them.

▪ Ask everyone to open their Mark's Gospels or Bibles at Mark 4. One of the leaders should read Mark 4:35-41.

▪ Work through the questions below to help the group explore the passage.

1. What hope of surviving the storm did the disciples have?

Almost none. The boat was "nearly swamped" (v 37). As they woke Jesus, they thought they were sure to drown (v 38).

2. What is so remarkable about the way in which Jesus calms the storm? (See Mark 4:39.)

He did it by speaking a few simple words to the forces of nature. The fact that Jesus instantly calmed not just the furious wind, but the huge waves as well – even though waves normally persist for hours after the wind dies down – shows that a miracle had taken place.

3. **The verses below (from Psalm 107) were a familiar song praising God for his power over the sea. The disciples would have known it well. As you read it, look for similarities with their experience in Mark 4:35-41.**

23 Others went out on the sea in ships;
    they were merchants on the mighty waters.

24 They saw the works of the LORD,
    his wonderful deeds in the deep.

25 For he spoke and stirred up a tempest
    that lifted high the waves.

26 They mounted up to the heavens and went down to the depths;
    in their peril their courage melted away.

27 They reeled and staggered like drunken men;
    they were at their wits' end.

28 Then they cried out to the LORD in their trouble,
    and he brought them out of their distress.

29 He stilled the storm to a whisper;
    the waves of the sea were hushed.

30 They were glad when it grew calm,
    and he guided them to their desired haven.

31 Let them give thanks to the LORD for his unfailing love
    and his wonderful deeds for men.

                                    Psalm 107:23-31

What similarities did you notice?

Group members may come up with some or all of the following. It doesn't matter if they miss one or two. The purpose is to see the close match between this Old Testament song about God, written around a thousand years before Jesus was born but sung regularly in the synagogue, and the events in Mark 4:35-41.

Psalm 107	Quote from psalm	The disciples' experience
Verse 23	"merchants on the mighty waters"	Several of the disciples had been fishermen.
Verse 24	"They saw the works of the LORD, his wonderful deeds in the deep"	The disciples saw Jesus calm the storm.
Verse 26	"They mounted up to the heavens and went down to the depths"	The furious squall threatened to sink their boat.
Verse 26	"in their peril their courage melted away"	The disciples were afraid.
Verse 27	"they were at their wits' end"	As the disciples woke Jesus, they were sure they couldn't do anything to save themselves.
Verse 28	"they cried out to the LORD in their trouble"	The disciples cried out to Jesus, although they didn't seem to expect him to be able to help.
Verses 28-29	"he brought them out of their distress. He stilled the storm to a whisper; the waves of the sea were hushed"	Jesus saved his disciples by calming both the wind and the waves.

4. The song and the story end in two different ways.
   (See Psalm 107:30 and Mark 4:41.)
   Why were the disciples still terrified after the storm had been calmed?

It is one thing to sing a praise song to God for his power over the wind and waves. It is quite another thing to be in a boat with a man who calms the sea and wind with a word – especially when seconds before you had rudely awakened him to complain that he didn't care! The awesome reality of Jesus' identity was coming home to the disciples.

LISTEN

▣ *(Page 13 in the group member's Handbook)* *Encourage the group to make notes and list questions they may have as they listen to the Bible talk or watch the DVD. There is space in the Handbook to make notes.*

"Who is this? Even the wind and the waves obey him!" (Mark 4:41)

▣ It's important to get the identity of Jesus right – otherwise we'll relate to him in the wrong way.

▣ Mark reveals the identity of Jesus by showing:

1. His power and authority to teach (Mark 1:21-22)

2. His power and authority over sickness (Mark 1:29-31, 32-34, 3:22)

3. His power and authority over nature (Mark 4:35-41; see also Psalm 107:23-31)

4. His power and authority over death (Mark 5:21-24, 35-43)

5. His power and authority to forgive sin (Mark 2:1-12)

▣ As God's Son and God's only chosen King, Jesus behaves with God's authority and displays God's power.

▣ *Note: Christianity Explored is based on the 1984 version of the New International Version (NIV). If you are using the 2011 revised NIV, you will find that "Ignoring what they said" in Mark 5:36 has been changed to "Overhearing what they said". Changing "ignoring" to "overhearing" does not affect the meaning of the text. The men who brought the news of the girl's death assumed there was nothing Jesus could now do. His message to Jairus, and his raising to life of the girl, show that the news of her death was no barrier to his power.*

DISCUSS

▣ (Page 14 in the group member's Handbook) Ask your group if there was anything that stood out or particularly struck them from the talk/DVD. This will help them to respond specifically to what they have just heard, before moving on to the group discussion questions.

What do you think of the evidence Mark gives us?

This question will show whether group members have understood the evidence Mark has been giving for the identity of Jesus. If they only mention one or two of the five examples from the talk/DVD, ask specifically about the others.

Optional supplementary question:

Jesus' enemies would have looked for every opportunity to discredit him. Why didn't they do so by proving that Jesus didn't have the power and authority he claimed?

Jesus' enemies would have exposed him as a fake if they could – but there are no examples of them even trying to do this. Instead of denying his power, they claimed it came from somewhere else. Jesus had power and authority over evil spirits (eg: Mark 1:23-28, 34; 2:10-12). The religious leaders who came from Jerusalem to investigate didn't deny this. Instead, they claimed that his power came from the devil ("Beelzebub") - an illogical claim that Jesus immediately showed to be wrong (Mark 3:22). The implication is that Jesus' enemies couldn't discredit Jesus because the evidence for his power and authority was both too strong and widely known.

What is your view of who Jesus is?

If some group members say they aren't sure who Jesus is, encourage them to keep reading Mark's Gospel and looking for the clues he gives us for the identity of Jesus. Some people may say that Jesus was just a particularly good teacher or a great man. If so, judge whether it would be appropriate to challenge that view, eg: "Surely a great man wouldn't claim to be able to forgive sins?"

▣ If you have time, now is the moment to answer another of the questions that were asked in the first session: "If you could ask God one question, and you knew it would be answered, what would it be?" See page 245 for guidance on common questions.

FOLLOW UP

📇 *(Page 15 in the group member's Handbook) Ask guests to complete the following study at home, and write down any questions they have. Before the next session, look through the study yourself so that you will be able to help group members with their questions.*

👁 **Read Mark 3:7 – 5:43**

📇 *Note: Christianity Explored is based on the 1984 version of the New International Version (NIV). If you are using the 2011 revised NIV, you will find that "sins and blasphemies" in Mark 3:28 has been changed to "sins and every slander". "Slander" is broader than "blasphemy", indicating that it is possible to be forgiven for speaking ill of God and man.*

1. In this passage Mark records Jesus doing four specific miracles:

a) calming a storm (Mark 4:35–41)

b) healing a demon-possessed man (Mark 5:1–20)

c) healing a sick woman (Mark 5:25–34)

d) raising a dead girl to life (Mark 5:35–43)

• What does Jesus show authority over in these events?

He shows authority over a) nature, b) evil spirits, c) illness and d) death.

• How does this add to what we've already seen about his power and authority in the earlier chapters?

We have previously seen Jesus' power and authority over evil spirits and illness. In confronting nature and death itself – by calming the storm and raising a dead girl to life – Jesus shows his power and authority in new situations.

2. When Jairus's daughter died, and all hope seemed to be lost (Mark 5:35), what did Jesus ask Jairus to do (verse 36)?

He told Jairus not to be afraid, but to have faith.

• Was that a "reasonable" thing to ask?

Everyone else had given up, so it was an astonishing thing to ask Jairus to do. It would not have seemed "reasonable" – instead it would seem foolish and cruel. But Jesus had already shown his power and authority over nature, evil spirits and illness – and he knew that he had authority over death as well. It would seem foolish and cruel coming from anyone else, but based on Jesus' past performance it was reasonable to ask Jairus to trust him.

3. Looking at all four events (see question 1) what are the different ways in which people respond to Jesus? See

a) Mark 4:40–41

b) Mark 5:15

c) Mark 5:27-28, 34

d) Mark 5:42

Do you see yourself in any of these responses?

a) The disciples are afraid.

b) The crowd who see him heal a demon-possessed man are afraid.

c) The woman has faith.

d) Jairus's family are amazed.

Do you have any questions about Mark 3:7 – 5:43?

The next session will start with group members being asked if they have any questions about the section of Mark they read at home. You will find help in answering difficult questions from Mark's Gospel in the appendix on page 237.

SIN
Why did Jesus come?

3

EXPLORE

▪ *Ask the guests to turn to Session 3 on page 17 of the Handbook.*

▪ *Ask if they have any questions from last session's Follow up. The appendix on page 237 lists common questions from Mark along with suggestions for answering them.*

▪ *Ask everyone to open their Mark's Gospels or Bibles at Mark 2. One of the leaders should read Mark 2:1-12.*

▪ *Work through the questions below to help the group explore the passage.*

---

1. A huge crowd had gathered to hear Jesus. Why?
What kind of reputation had he built up in these early days?
(Look at Mark 1:27–28, 32–34, 45 for clues.)

Jesus' teaching and healing had amazed people, and news about him was spreading.

---

2. Why do you think the four friends decided to bring the paralyzed man to Jesus?

They must have thought Jesus would be able to heal him.

---

3. What is the first thing Jesus says to the paralyzed man (Mark 2:5)?
Is that surprising? Why or why not?

Jesus says: "Son, your sins are forgiven". That is very surprising, considering that the man was lowered through the roof to be healed, not to have his sins forgiven.

But we have seen (in last session's talk/DVD) that Jesus believes that our relationship with God is far more important than our physical health. (The seriousness of sin will be the focus of today's talk/DVD.)

4. Why were the teachers of the law so annoyed by what Jesus said? (See Mark 2:6–7.)

Jesus is claiming to do what they believe only God can do (Mark 2:7), so they conclude that he is blaspheming.

5. Had they reached the right conclusion?

Yes and no. Yes, only God has the ultimate right and authority to forgive our sin, since all sin is an offence against God*, and all forgiveness must come from Him.

No, Jesus isn't blaspheming, since as the "Son of Man" (verse 10) he has the authority of God (see next question). "Son of Man" was a title Jesus often used about himself. This title is used in other places in the Bible and refers to God's only chosen King, to whom he gives authority. (It comes from the Old Testament book of Daniel where the Son of Man came from heaven and was given eternal rule over the whole world. See "Why did Jesus call himself the Son of Man?" in the appendix on page 237.)

* For example, although David had wronged Bathsheba's husband, Uriah, when he committed adultery with Bathsheba, he prayed: "Against you, you only, have I sinned" (Psalm 51:4). Don't use this example unless a group member asks – it may be an unnecessary complication for the rest of the group.

6. How do we know that Jesus has authority to forgive sin? (See Mark 2:8–12.)

He showed his authority by healing the man instantly and completely.

LISTEN

(Page 19 in the group member's Handbook) Encourage the group to make notes and list questions they may have as they listen to the Bible talk or watch the DVD. There is space in the Handbook to make notes.

"I have not come to call the righteous, but sinners." (Mark 2:17)

- The reason the world is not the way it's supposed to be is because we are not the way we're supposed to be.

- Jesus tells us that "sin" comes "from within", from our "hearts" (Mark 7:20-22).

- Each of us has a heart problem. We often treat each other and our world in a shameful way, and we treat God in that way too.

- We should love God with all our heart, soul, mind and strength. But we never manage to do this.

- We've all rebelled against God, our loving Creator. The Bible calls this "sin".

- Jesus came to cure our heart problem, the problem of our sin. He came for people who realize they're bad, not for people who think they're good.

- Jesus lovingly warns us about hell because he does not want us to go there. Our sin means we're all in danger, whether we realize it or not (Mark 9:43-47).

Note: Christianity Explored is based on the 1984 version of the New International Version (NIV). If you are using the 2011 revised NIV, you will find that throughout Mark 7:1-23 "unclean" has been changed to "defiled". The replacement of "unclean" with "defiled" is only intended to underline that this is a Jewish ceremonial issue, as verses 3-4 show. The Pharisees and teachers of the law wrongly thought it possible to be spiritually contaminated, or defiled by contact with non-Jews. In Mark 9:42-47 "sin" has been changed to "stumble" each time. "Stumble" is probably a better translation of the Greek than "sin". But we must explain that what Jesus has in mind here is not accidental stumbling, but actual sin which causes a moral fall.

DISCUSS

🔲 *(Page 20 in the group member's Handbook)* Ask your group if there was
anything that stood out or particularly struck them from the talk/DVD. This
will help them to respond specifically to what they have just heard, before
moving on to the group discussion questions.

**Read Mark 9:43-47. Why do you think Jesus used such extreme language
when talking about the need to avoid hell?**

Jesus knows that our relationship with God is far more important than anything
else. Jesus lovingly warns his disciples about hell because he does not want them to
go there. Hell means eternal separation from God's blessing. Hell is the place where
we face God's judgment for our rebellion against him. So we need to take this issue
seriously. Hell is so serious that Jesus uses extreme examples to make his point. If we
find them ridiculously extreme, it's probably because we underestimate the seriousness of the heart problem that Jesus talks about in Mark 7:14-23.

Jesus believed in hell. Should we? Why or why not?

In the 21st century many people either dismiss hell as a myth, or make jokes about
it. But Jesus was very serious about the reality and horror of hell. He lovingly warns
us so that we can be rescued from hell, a threat he took so seriously that he was
ready to die to save us from it. (Explain that we'll be exploring Jesus' death in more
detail next week.)

**Imagine that all of your thoughts, words and actions were displayed for
everyone to see. How would you feel?**

This question helps people to think about the detail of their own lives without
them having to reveal personal issues. Hopefully it will help them to understand
that everyone falls short of God's standards (in fact most will admit that they don't
even meet their own standards). This means we're all sinners – we all have a heart
problem – and that we all need to be rescued.

🔲 *If you have time, now is the moment to answer another of the questions
that were asked in the first session: "If you could ask God one question,
and you knew it would be answered, what would it be?" See page 245 for
guidance on common questions.*

FOLLOW UP

🔲 *(Page 21 in the group member's Handbook) Ask guests to complete the following study at home, and write down any questions they have. Before the next session, look through the study yourself so that you will be able to help group members with their questions.*

👁 **Read Mark 6:1 – 8:29**

> **1. In the earlier chapters (1-5) Mark has built up a picture of Jesus' power and authority. He's shown us various miracles: healing the sick, casting out demons, raising the dead, calming a storm.**
>
> **How does this passage (Mark 6:1 – 8:29) add to that picture? (See Mark 6:32–44, 47–48; 7:31–37; 8:1–10, 22–26.)**

🔲 Jesus is able to feed vast crowds of people from a handful of food (Mark 6:32-44; 8:1-10).

🔲 He is able to heal the deaf and mute, and also the blind (Mark 7:31-37; 8:22-26).

🔲 He is able to walk on water (Mark 6:47-48).

Note: The passages here are full of Old Testament imagery, pointing to the fact that Jesus is the Rescuer promised in the Old Testament. Depending on your group, it may or may not be appropriate to explain those links to them (see below*). Alternatively, you could simply mention that since the disciples (and many of the crowds) were Jewish, they would recognize echoes of the Old Testament in the things Jesus did.

* "like sheep without a shepherd" (Mark 6:34) – In Ezekiel 34, Israel is described as being like sheep without a shepherd because her leaders had not done their job properly (Ezekiel 34:1–6). As a result, God promised to come himself to rescue his people (Ezekiel 34:16). Jesus is that rescuer, acting as God's shepherd by feeding the sheep in a miraculous way (Mark 6:30–44; 8:1–10), as God himself had done when rescuing Israel from Egypt (Exodus 16:32–35). Jesus is also said to "pass by" the disciples as he walks on water, in language reminiscent of God passing by Moses at the time he received the stone tablets (Mark 6:48; cf. Exodus 34:1–9).

2. Jesus saw the large crowd in Mark 6:34 as "sheep without a shepherd". What did he do about it?

When Jesus saw the crowd, he "had compassion on them" (v 34) and so he began to teach them.

• If Jesus looked at the faces of people in a busy town today, do you think he would feel the same? Why / why not?

The crowd in Mark 6 were Jewish, so the Jewish religious leaders should have been "shepherds" caring for them*. But most of the religious leaders failed to be the "shepherds" God wanted them to be, so this crowd were "sheep without a shepherd". In a similar way, in any crowd of people today there are likely to be many who have no clue about the good news of Jesus. Some of them may even attend church services, but have never heard the gospel message clearly explained.

* See the note on page 89 for more on "sheep without a shepherd" (from Ezekiel 34).

• Do you feel the need to have Jesus as your shepherd?

This part of the question is designed to encourage group members to reflect that Jesus wants to be our Shepherd and teacher in the same way.

3. Write down the very different reactions to Jesus' preaching and miracles:

a) in his home synagogue (Mark 6:1-6)

b) among people generally (Mark 6:14-15, 53-56; 7:37)

c) from the disciples (Mark 6:51-52)

d) from the religious leaders (Mark 8:11).

• Why do you think people responded so differently?

The way people responded to Jesus seemed to be based on what they already thought about him.

a) The people from his home town, Nazareth, had seen Jesus grow up so they thought they already knew all about him. They were suspicious of him.

b) Elsewhere, Jesus had a great reputation. People had heard of his miracles and crowded to him hoping to see more of the same.

c) The disciples, who know Jesus best, do not know what to make of him. They still don't understand who he is.

d) The religious leaders are offended by Jesus, and want to "test" him. In spite of all the miracles, the Pharisees want him to do something spectacular – just for them.

> • **Do you identify particularly with one of those groups?**

This question is designed to help group members reflect on their own response to Jesus.

> **4. Read Jesus' question in Mark 8:29. How would you have answered this before you started *Christianity Explored*?**
>
> **Now that you're halfway through Mark's Gospel, and have read about the amazing things that Jesus said and did, has your answer changed?**
>
> **If you still have questions about the identity of Jesus, write them below.**

The three parts of question 4 are designed to encourage group members to reflect on what they have learned so far, particularly about the identity of Jesus.

> **Do you have any questions about Mark 6:1 – 8:29?**

The next session will start with group members being asked if they have any questions about the section of Mark they read at home. You will find help in answering difficult questions from Mark's Gospel in the appendix on page 237.

THE CROSS

Why did Jesus die?

4

EXPLORE

▪ Ask the guests to turn to *Session 4* on page 25 of the *Handbook*.

▪ Ask if they have any questions from last session's *Follow up*. The appendix on page 237 lists common questions from Mark along with suggestions for answering them.

▪ Ask everyone to open their Mark's Gospels or Bibles at Mark 8. One of the leaders should read *Mark 8:22-33*.

▪ Work through the questions below to help the group explore the passage.

1. Generally speaking, who do people today believe Jesus is? What do they base these views on?

You might ask your group to imagine that they are conducting a survey outside a popular local shop. What answers do they think they would get to the question: "Who do you think Jesus is?"

Answers are likely to be both positive and negative. They may include: a good man, a wise teacher, a prophet, a trouble-maker, a mythical person who didn't really exist…

These views can be based on things they've heard others say, the media, Sunday school, religious TV channels, etc.

2. Peter's statement in Mark 8:29 seems to form a turning point in Mark's Gospel (see Mark 8:31). What did Peter say, and why do you think it was so important?

Peter said that Jesus is the Christ (God's only chosen King). His moment of recognition was important because none of the twelve disciples had understood this so far, despite all that Jesus had said and done. Now that they recognized the identity of Jesus, he could begin to explain to them what would happen to him as God's King.

3. Once the identity of Jesus was clear (Mark 8:29), he went on to explain his mission in Mark 8:31-32. Why do you think Peter rebuked Jesus? (See Mark 8:32-33.)

Peter was appalled to hear that Jesus was willing to suffer, be rejected and die before rising again. He was driven to talk Jesus out of his mission by having in mind "the things of men", merely human priorities. This may have meant that Peter wanted Jesus to continue healing the sick and raising the dead, so that his popularity would grow. It may also have meant that Peter hoped that God's King (the Christ) would drive out the occupying Roman forces so that the country was free.

4. Mark records the two-stage healing of the blind man in Mark 8:22-26. He went from seeing *nothing* (Mark 8:22) to seeing *something* (Mark 8:24) to seeing *everything* (Mark 8:25).
How clearly are the disciples "seeing" the identity and mission of Jesus in Mark 8:27-33?

If your group struggle to answer this question, ask: "Peter has seen Jesus' identity in verse 29. Has he seen Jesus' mission yet?"

Peter appears to be seeing with perfect clarity in Mark 8:29 – he gets Jesus' identity right. But when Peter rebukes Jesus in verse 32, it shows that he is not seeing the nature of Jesus' mission clearly. Peter sees "something" but he is not yet seeing "everything"– so Jesus warns him, and the other disciples, not to say anything about him being the Christ (v 30).

5. Jesus told Peter he had in mind "the things of men". What phrase did Jesus use to describe his suffering and death (Mark 8:33)?

"The things of God".

What does this tell us about his mission?

Jesus was confirming that his mission came from God. It was God's plan that he would suffer and die.

6. In Mark 8:29, Jesus asks: "But what about you? Who do you say I am?"
Are you able to give a definite answer to this question yet?
If so, how would you answer and why?

This question is designed to reveal where the group members are in their own view of Jesus.

Rather than pressing them for an answer, it may be more appropriate for your group to reflect on this and for you to discuss it one-to-one later.

LISTEN

(Page 28 in the group member's Handbook) Encourage the group to make notes and list questions they may have as they listen to the Bible talk or watch the DVD. There is space in the Handbook to make notes.

"For even the Son of Man did not come to be served, but to serve, and to give his life as a ransom for many." (Mark 10:45)

- Jesus' death on a cross wasn't a tragic waste of life. It was a rescue.

- Jesus taught his followers that he must be killed. He came to "give his life as a ransom for many" (Mark 10:45).

- As Jesus was dying on the cross, darkness came over the whole land. God was acting in anger to punish sin.

- On the cross, Jesus was in some way "forsaken" or abandoned by God, as God punished sin.

- Jesus gave himself up as a substitute, to be punished on our behalf. He bore the punishment that our sin deserves, so that we can be rescued.

- When Jesus died, the curtain in the temple was torn in two from top to bottom (Mark 15:38). Because of the cross, the way is now open for people to approach God.

- The people who saw Jesus die reacted in different ways:

  - The soldiers missed what was happening.

  - The religious leaders were convinced they already knew the way to God.

  - The Roman governor, Pontius Pilate, gave in to the crowd.

  - The Roman centurion recognized the identity of Jesus: "Surely this man was the Son of God!" (Mark 15:39).

- *Note: Christianity Explored is based on the 1984 version of the New International Version (NIV). If you are using the 2011 revised NIV, you will find that "two robbers" in Mark 15:27 has been changed to "two rebels". The two who were crucified either side of Jesus may have been rebels against the state, rather than robbers. Irrespective of this, at the most basic theological level, all sin is rebellion against God.*

DISCUSS

- *(Page 29 in the group member's Handbook) Ask your group if there was anything that stood out or particularly struck them from the talk/DVD. This will help them to respond specifically to what they have just heard, before moving on to the group discussion questions.*

How would you feel if someone else deliberately took the punishment for something serious you had done wrong?

This question could bring out a number of reactions including:

- relieved: that you won't be punished.

- guilty: that someone has taken the blame for something they didn't do.

- bad: for the person who suffered.

- angry: that the wrong person has taken the blame for someone else's wrongdoing.

- grateful: that they've taken your punishment for you.

Jesus said he came "to give his life as a ransom for many" (Mark 10:45). What's your reaction to this?

This takes the issues behind the previous "hypothetical" question, and makes them real and personal. Jesus did take "the punishment for something serious" – our sin.

You may want to explain to the group that the "ransom" Jesus talks about wasn't money paid to a kidnapper. In those days a slave could be given their freedom if a "ransom" was paid.

Which of the reactions to Jesus' death is most like your reaction?

Some people may not want to answer this in front of others. If no one wants to answer, you could start the conversation by asking what they think their friends might say.

This question gives an opportunity to apply the four reactions directly to people's own situations:

- The soldiers were so busy they missed what was happening right in front of them: Are we so absorbed with our busy lives that we don't take time to really think about why Jesus came, and our response to that?

- The religious leaders thought they already knew the way to God: Even if we're very "religious", none of us are good enough for God. All of us sin, and none of us can deal with our sin by ourselves. Religion can't save us. Only Jesus can.

- Pontius Pilate went with the crowd: It's very easy to give in to peer pressure. Choosing to follow Jesus would mean going his way instead of following the crowd. Are we ready to do that?

- The Roman centurion recognized who Jesus is: We don't know much about this centurion. We know he got Jesus' identity right, but we don't know what he did after that. Recognizing who Jesus is isn't all we need to do – we then need to put our trust in him to rescue us from the problem of sin and help us live as his followers.

■ *If you have time, now is the moment to answer another of the questions that were asked in the first session: "If you could ask God one question, and you knew it would be answered, what would it be?" See page 245 for guidance on common questions.*

■ *Give out invitations to the day away, and explain that this will be happening after session 6 of the course. See Section 3 on page 129 for details of the day away.*

FOLLOW UP

■ *(Page 30 in the group member's Handbook) Ask guests to complete the following study at home, and write down any questions they have. Before the next session, look through the study yourself so that you will be able to help group members with their questions.*

👁 Read Mark 8:30 – 10:52

(Note that "Son of Man" is Jesus' way of referring to himself.)

1. Jesus directly predicts his own death and resurrection three times (Mark 8:31, 9:31 and 10:33-34).
What does he say "must" and "will" happen?

He must suffer, be rejected by the religious leaders, be killed and, three days later, rise again (Mark 8:31).

He will be betrayed, killed and, three days later, rise again (Mark 9:31).

He will be betrayed. He will be handed over to the Gentiles* by the religious leaders in Jerusalem. He will be mocked, spat on, flogged and killed. Three days later he will rise again (Mark 10:33-34).

* In this case the "Gentiles" (non-Jews) are the Roman authorities.

2. In Mark 8:31 Jesus said he "must" die. Why did he have to die?
(See Mark 10:45.)

Jesus came to serve by dying – giving his life as a ransom for many.

3. What did Jesus say that following him would mean? (See Mark 8:34.)

He said his followers must deny themselves, take up their cross and follow him.

4. Each time Jesus predicts his own death and resurrection, Mark records the disciples' response – or lack of it. (See Mark 8:32–33; 9:32–35; 10:35–45.) How do the disciples respond in each case?

Each time Jesus tells his disciples about his death, an event immediately follows that shows that the disciples have not understood his teaching:

- Peter rebukes Jesus because he hasn't understood that Jesus must suffer and die. Peter has in mind "the things of men", not God.

- The disciples argue about who is the greatest (Mark 9:34). They haven't understood Jesus' teaching on denying themselves (Mark 8:34).

- James and John want to sit next to Jesus in his glory, because – again – they haven't learned to deny themselves and put others first.

5. In Mark 8:29 Peter recognizes that Jesus is the Christ, God's only chosen King. In taking Jesus aside and rebuking him (Mark 8:32), Peter is not treating Jesus as God's King.
How do you think you have treated Jesus?
How would you feel about Jesus being King in every area of your life?

This question is designed to help group members reflect on their own attitudes to Jesus.

Do you have any questions about Mark 8:30 – 10:52?

The next session will start with group members being asked if they have any questions about the section of Mark they read at home. You will find help in answering difficult questions from Mark's Gospel in the appendix on page 237.

RESURRECTION
Why did Jesus rise?

5

EXPLORE

- Ask the guests to turn to Session 5 on page 33 of the Handbook.

- Ask if they have any questions from last session's Follow up. The appendix on page 237 lists common questions from Mark along with suggestions for answering them.

- Ask everyone to open their Mark's Gospels or Bibles at Mark 14. One of the leaders should read Mark 14:27-31.

- Work through the questions below to help the group explore the passage.

---

1. In this section Jesus is speaking to his disciples. What predictions did Jesus make? (See Mark 14:27, 28 and 30.)

In verse 27 Jesus predicted that the disciples would all fall away (ie: turn away from Jesus).

In verse 28 Jesus predicted that he would rise to life, and then go to Galilee (where the disciples would join him).

In verse 30 Jesus predicted that during the night, before the rooster (cockerel) crowed twice (ie: before daybreak), Peter would disown Jesus three times.

---

2. In what ways does Peter disagree with Jesus' predictions? (See Mark 14:29, 31.)

In verse 29 Peter said that he would not fall away (turn away from Jesus), even if all the other disciples did.

In verse 31 Peter said that he would never disown Jesus, even if it meant dying with him.

3. In Mark 14:27 Jesus quoted from the Old Testament (Zechariah 13:7) to explain what he was about to suffer, and why the disciples would scatter.
How do we know that Jesus fully intended to gather the "sheep" who would be scattered by his death? (See Mark 14:28 and Mark 16:6-7.)

We know from Mark 14:28 that Jesus was as sure about rising from death as he was about dying. We also know from Mark 16:7 that Jesus had told the disciples they would see him, alive and well, in Galilee.

4. Which of Jesus' predictions did Peter pay attention to?
Which did he ignore?

Peter focused on Jesus' prediction that the disciples would all fall away – and insisted that he wouldn't. But he seemed to ignore what Jesus said about rising again and going ahead of them into Galilee.

5. Jesus had spoken plainly and repeatedly about his resurrection from death. (See Mark 8:31, 9:30-31, 10:32-34.)
Did the disciples understand what this meant?
If not, why didn't they ask Jesus about it? (See Mark 9:32.)

Mark 9:32 tells us that the disciples didn't understand what Jesus meant but were afraid to ask him about it.

The whole mission of Jesus – his rejection, suffering and death – was beyond the grasp of the disciple's minds. It was difficult for them to come to terms with these terrible aspects of his death – and even more difficult to grasp the concept of him rising from the dead.

It is important for group members to see that Mark doesn't present the resurrection as something people readily accept, but as something truly mind-blowing.

(This question is designed to draw attention to the consistency of Jesus' teaching about his resurrection – and the slowness of the disciples to come to terms with the scope of his mission. In this session we will see that, just as he said he would, Jesus rose from death (Mark 16:6-7).)

LISTEN

(Page 36 in the group member's Handbook) *Encourage the group to make notes and list questions they may have as they listen to the Bible talk or watch the DVD. There is space in the Handbook to make notes.*

"He has risen! ... just as he told you." (Mark 16:6-7)

- Jesus repeatedly claimed that he would be raised to life on the third day after his death.

- Jesus really did die: the women, Joseph of Arimathea, the Roman centurion and Pontius Pilate were all certain that Jesus had died.

- 36 hours later, the huge, heavy stone covering the entrance to his tomb had been rolled away.

- A young man in a white robe told the women that Jesus had risen from death. He also said that the disciples would see Jesus in Galilee, just as he had told them before he died.

- Jesus appeared to his disciples on at least ten separate occasions after his death. He also appeared to more than 500 people at the same time.

- It is not only the disciples who will see the risen Jesus. We will see him too.

- The resurrection guarantees that one day we will all be physically raised from the dead. And Jesus will be our Judge on that day.

- Jesus died to pay for sin, and rose from death to prove that sin was truly paid for. If we put our trust in Jesus, all of our sin will be fully and finally forgiven.

- Because of the resurrection, we can trust Jesus with our own death. Are we ready to meet him?

DISCUSS

(Page 37 in the group member's Handbook) Ask your group if there was anything that stood out or particularly struck them from the talk/DVD. This will help them to respond specifically to what they have just heard, before moving on to the group discussion questions.

> **"For God has set a day when he will judge the world with justice by the man he has appointed. He has given proof of this to all men by raising him from the dead" (Acts 17:31). What's your reaction to this?**

There are two strong statements in this session that your group may find hard to believe or be unwilling to accept: that Jesus rose again, and that Jesus will return to judge everyone. The answers to this question will help you see what stage your group have reached in their response to Jesus.

If some group members don't believe that they deserve judgment, or think they will be judged as "good", they haven't yet understood the seriousness of sin.

If they are worried that they will "fail" the judgment, that shows they understand their heart problem – but do remind them that Jesus' death and resurrection proves that their sin, however serious, can be forgiven. Judgment is not a fearful thing for those whose trust is in the Judge. Encourage them to come to the next session to hear the good news about why God can accept us.

If group members struggle to believe/accept that Jesus will return as Judge, look again at Mark 8. Every prediction Jesus made in verse 31 came true. Is it unreasonable to believe that his prediction in verse 38 will also come true? Encourage them to read through the account again and to think about it in their own time.

If they believe everything else about Jesus up to this point, then you might like to explain that his return is logical – having conquered sin and death, he will not leave the world in its sinful struggle forever.

> **Do you believe Jesus rose from the dead? Why or why not?**

This question is designed to stimulate a general discussion about the evidence as well as clarifying what the group members believe about the resurrection.

If you have time, now is the moment to answer another of the questions that were asked in the first session: "If you could ask God one question, and you knew it would be answered, what would it be?" See page 245 for guidance on common questions.

📋 *Remind the group about the day away after Session 6, and give out invitations to any who were missing last time or who have lost theirs.*

FOLLOW UP

📋 *(Page 38 in the group member's Handbook) Ask guests to complete the following study at home, and write down any questions they have. Before the next session, look through the study yourself so that you will be able to help group members with their questions.*

👁 **Read Mark 11:1-33**

1. What is the crowd's attitude towards Jesus as he arrives in Jerusalem? (See Mark 11:8–10.)

They are respectful, joyful and hopeful – some spread their cloaks on the road, others spread branches. They welcome Jesus with shouts of praise.

Note: "Hosanna" is a Hebrew word meaning "Save us!"

2. The Old Testament prophet Zechariah wrote about a time when someone would ride into Jerusalem (also called Zion) on a colt.

> Rejoice greatly, O Daughter of Zion!
> Shout, Daughter of Jerusalem!
> See, your king comes to you,
> righteous and having salvation,
> gentle and riding on a donkey,
> on a colt, the foal of a donkey.
> *Zechariah 9:9*

What would the crowd understand about Jesus when he arrived in that way?

Zechariah prophesied about a time when Israel's King would arrive in Jerusalem (Zion). The King was righteous and had the ability to save his people. He wouldn't arrive on a war-horse, but on a colt, the foal of a donkey. So this event in Mark 11 signalled that Jesus was that King (his identity) and had come to save (his mission).

👁 **Read Mark 12:1 – 13:37**

---

3. How do the religious leaders respond to Jesus in Mark 11:18 and 12:12?

They fear him because of his popularity with the crowd (Mark 11:18).

They look for an opportunity to arrest Jesus because they know his parable is about them and their plan to kill him (Mark 12:1-11).

---

4. How do these leaders treat Jesus as a result of their fear of him? (See Mark 11:27–33; 12:13–17.)

They question Jesus' authority.

They are two-faced: they flatter him, but seek to trap him with trick questions.

---

5. The Sadducees were a group of religious leaders who did not believe in resurrection. In Mark 12:18-23 they tried to make Jesus look foolish with their question about the resurrection.
What did Jesus say was the real reason for their disbelief? (See Mark 12:24.)

Jesus said they did not know either the Scriptures (the Old Testament) or the power of God.

---

6. What other criticism does Jesus make of religious leaders? (See Mark 12:38-40.)

He talks about their pride and conceit and their hypocrisy – their concern only with appearance and reputation. They care about themselves, instead of caring for widows.

7. A few days later the mood of the crowd had turned. Led by their religious leaders they demanded the death of Jesus (see Mark 15:9-13). Does it surprise you that it is possible to be respected, even religious, and still reject Jesus?
   Why or why not?

This question will help to show whether group members have understood the difference between being religious (ie: living a "good" life, keeping religious rules, attending church...) and believing in and following Jesus.

Do you have any questions about Mark 11:1 – 13:37?

The next session will start with group members being asked if they have any questions about the section of Mark they read at home. You will find help in answering difficult questions from Mark's Gospel in the appendix on page 237.

GRACE

How can God accept us?

6

EXPLORE

■ *Ask the guests to turn to Session 6 on page 41 of the Handbook.*

■ *Ask if they have any questions from last session's Follow up. The appendix on page 237 lists common questions from Mark along with suggestions for answering them.*

■ *Ask everyone to open their Mark's Gospels or Bibles at Mark 10. One of the leaders should read Mark 10:13-16.*

■ *Work through the questions below to help the group explore the passage.*

> **1. From all we have seen of Jesus, why do you think people would bring their children to him? (See Mark 10:13 and 16.)**

They brought their children to Jesus in the hope that he would touch them (v 13) and bless them (v 16).

> **2. We are not told why the disciples rebuked those who brought their children to Jesus. What might have been the reason for their intolerance? (See Mark 9:33-34.)**

Answers may include:

■ The disciples had been arguing about their own greatness. Meeting the needs of children may have been low on their priorities.

■ They may have believed that Jesus was too important, busy or tired to be disturbed by "unimportant" children. (Note: though children may have been loved by their families, they had little status in first-century Israel.)

3. Read Mark 9:33-37.

In Mark 10:14 we are told that Jesus was indignant with the disciples. Are you surprised that he reacted so strongly? Why or why not?

Some may be surprised that Jesus is capable of being unashamedly indignant – but it is consistent with his love of what is good, and his appropriate anger at what is wrong.

It's not surprising that Jesus was exasperated with the disciples, since he had already given them training on welcoming children in Mark 9:35-37.

4. Read Mark 10:14-15. How do we know that Jesus is not just talking about actual *children* belonging to the kingdom of God?

In Mark 10:14 Jesus says that the kingdom of God (the place of God's presence and blessing) belongs to *such* as these. In Mark 10:15 he speaks of anyone receiving the kingdom of God *like* a little child. Jesus is using the children as a picture of those who receive the gift of God's kingdom.

5. Read Mark 10:16. The little children did nothing to earn acceptance by Jesus. All they did was come to him and he took them in his arms. What is the significance of this for our entry into God's kingdom? (See Mark 10:15.)

Jesus says that those who will not receive God's kingdom like little children will be unable to enter it. It is difficult for adults, who are used to having to earn acceptance with others, to simply come empty-handed to Jesus. But that is the only way into God's kingdom.

LISTEN

🔲 *(Page 43 in the group member's Handbook) Encourage the group to make notes and list questions they may have as they listen to the Bible talk or watch the DVD. There is space in the Handbook to make notes.*

"I tell you the truth, anyone who will not receive the kingdom of God like a little child will never enter it." (Mark 10:15)

- If God asked "Why should I give you eternal life?", what would you say?

- The rich young man wanted to know how to be good enough for God.

- We can never do enough to inherit eternal life.

- Nothing we do can cure our heart problem.

- But we can receive eternal life as a free gift – paid for by the death of Jesus. This is grace – God's undeserved gift to us.

- We are more sinful than we ever realized, but more loved than we ever dreamed.

DISCUSS

- *(Page 44 in the group member's Handbook) Ask your group if there was anything that stood out or particularly struck them from the talk/DVD. This will help them to respond specifically to what they have just heard, before moving on to the group discussion questions.*

"What must I do to inherit eternal life?" (Mark 10:17) How would you answer that question?

This question is designed to clarify the group's understanding of grace. There is nothing we can do, other than trust entirely in what Jesus has done. If group members still mention living a good life and doing religious things, gently point them back to Mark 10:15.

"You are more sinful than you ever realized, but more loved than you ever dreamed." How do you respond to this?

This question is designed to provoke reflection on these two core aspects of the gospel – hopeless human sinfulness and God's gracious love revealed in Jesus. Look out for defensive responses to the charge of personal sinfulness, which may call for a return to Mark 7:20-23.

Although it's important that the group clearly understand the hopelessness of trying to "earn" eternal life, don't end the discussion there. Emphasize the wonder of grace – God's undeserved gift to us, paid for by the death of Jesus.

> **Has grace made a difference to the view of God you had in Session 1?**

This question is designed to draw out the two sides of God's character – that he is both just and merciful. God's justice means that he will not leave sin unpunished. God's mercy means that he does not treat us as we deserve, but instead he lovingly sent his Son, Jesus, to save us from our sin.

Some group members may have started this course believing that God is just a strict disciplinarian who makes rules for us to follow. Others may have seen him as automatically "welcoming everyone into heaven", except for "really bad" people. An understanding of grace will help group members to have a fuller and more biblical view of God's character.

🔲 *If you have time, now is the moment to answer another of the questions that were asked in the first session: "If you could ask God one question, and you knew it would be answered, what would it be?" See page 245 for guidance on common questions.*

🔲 *Remind the group about the day away, and confirm any arrangements.*

FOLLOW UP

🔲 *(Page 45 in the group member's Handbook) Ask guests to complete the following study at home, and write down any questions they have. Before the next session, look through the study yourself so that you will be able to help group members with their questions.*

👁 **Read Mark 14:1-72**

> **1. Mark tells us about Jesus' last night with his disciples, and his trial by the Jewish court, the Sanhedrin. How do we know from Mark's account that Jesus' death was not a mistake or accident? (See Mark 14:12–26, 27-31, 48–49, 61–62.)**

These events show that Jesus predicted and prepared for his death. He was in total control.

- **Mark 14:12-26:** Jesus knew that the Passover meal would be his last meal with the disciples, and had prepared for it in advance. He also knew that one of the disciples would betray him.

- **Mark 14:27-31:** Jesus predicted that he would die the next day (the Passover meal was on a Thursday evening – Jesus was crucified on the Friday). He knew that the disciples would desert him, and that Peter would disown him.

- **Mark 14:48-49:** Jesus knew that his arrest and execution would fulfil prophecies made in the Old Testament Scriptures.

- **Mark 14:61-62:** Jesus knew that his death would not be the end. He would sit at the right hand of God the Father ("the Mighty One"), and return "on the clouds of heaven".

> **2. Jesus knew that it was his mission to die. Does that mean that death was easy for him? (See Mark 14:33–36; 15:34.)**

No. Jesus' agony in the garden of Gethsemane, and his cry on the cross ("My God, my God, why have you forsaken me?"), show just how hard his death was.

It's possible that a group member may say: "If Jesus' death was so hard, then surely, if God is God, there must have been another way to solve this problem". Jesus' prayer in Gethsemane answers this question decisively: "everything is possible for you. Take this cup from me. Yet not what I will, but what you will" (Mark 14:36). The fact that Jesus' death on the cross still happens after his prayer strongly suggests that there is no other way to solve the problem: it is that serious.

👁 **Read Mark 15:1 – 16:8**

> **3. At the moment that Jesus died, something happened in the temple on the other side of the city (Mark 15:38). What happened?**

The temple curtain was torn in two from top to bottom.

> • **The temple curtain was like a big "No entry" sign. It showed that people were cut off from God because of their sins. Why do you think Mark records what happened to this curtain?**

The curtain had been a symbol of the barrier between people and God. It was torn in two as a symbol of how Jesus' death opens the way to God.

4. In Mark 14:50 we see the disciples deserting Jesus. In Mark 14:66–72 we see Peter repeatedly disowning him. Given all that Jesus had said about his death, why do you think they responded like this?

They were afraid. They didn't understand that Jesus was in control of everything that happened. They still didn't understand that Jesus had to die and rise.

5. A Roman centurion was in charge of the crucifixion. What did he say when Jesus died (Mark 15:39)?

The centurion said: "Surely this man was the Son of God!"

• Why did he say this – and why is it surprising?

He said this because he saw the way that Jesus died (Mark 15:37).

It is surprising because he was the Roman centurion directly responsible for Jesus' death – and yet it was his death that made clear to this man who Jesus was. (He was also a Gentile. The Jews believed that Gentiles would not be saved.)

6. Grace is when God treats us in the opposite way to what we deserve. It is an undeserved gift.
Peter had disowned Jesus three times (Mark 14:66-72).
How do you think Peter would have felt when he was given the message of Mark 16:7? Why?

Peter must have felt amazed to be included, and thrilled to be forgiven. He may also have been nervous about seeing Jesus.

• The grace Jesus shows to Peter is a picture of the grace now offered to us. How will you respond to the gift Jesus offers?

The final part of the question is designed to help group members think about their own response to all they have learned and read about God's grace.

Do you have any questions about Mark 14:1 – 16:8?

The next session will start with group members being asked if they have any questions about the section of Mark they read at home. You will find help in answering difficult questions from Mark's Gospel in the appendix on page 237.

One specific question group members may ask is why the Follow up passage ends at Mark 16:8 rather than Mark 16:20. See page 244 for a comment on Mark 16:9-20.

DAY AWAY

The day away is an important part of the *Christianity Explored* course as it will give your group members an opportunity to reflect on what they have learned and consider the implications for their own lives. The day away material is designed to be used in between Sessions 6 and 7 of the course.

The following themes will be covered:

1: THE SOWER: Listen carefully
We must listen to Jesus, and act on what we hear.

2: JAMES AND JOHN: Ask humbly
Following Jesus is about service, not status. We need to ask Jesus for mercy, not a reward.

3: HEROD: Choose wisely
Ignoring Jesus' call to repent and believe will eventually earn us the rejection of Jesus.

Spending a day together allows more time for reflection and for personal testimonies – either from leaders or other members of the church family. It will also give the group time to observe how you and your co-leaders live out your own faith in Jesus.

You will find all the material for the day away in Section 3 of this Leader's manual, starting on page 129.

COME AND DIE

What does it mean to follow Jesus?

7

EXPLORE

- Ask the guests to turn to Session 7 on page 57 of the Handbook.

- Ask if they have any questions from last session's Follow up. The appendix on page 237 lists common questions from Mark along with suggestions for answering them.

- Ask everyone to open their Mark's Gospels or Bibles at Mark 1. One of the leaders should read Mark 1:14-15.

- Work through the questions below to help the group explore the passage.

1. **All through *Christianity Explored* we have heard about the good news. In Mark 1:14-15 it's mentioned twice. But to understand the good news, we need to understand the "bad news" first. What is the bad news in the following verses?**

- **Mark 7:20-23** We are naturally sinful people and sin comes from within us.

- **Mark 9:43-47** Sin left untreated will take us to hell.

- **Mark 10:26-27** It is impossible for us to save ourselves from our sin.

2. **"Jesus went ... proclaiming the good news" (Mark 1:14). What is the good news answer to these session titles from the course?**

- **Why did Jesus come?** The good news is that Jesus came to call sinners (Mark 2:17), and to cure our heart problem by giving his life as a ransom (Mark 10:45).

- **Why did Jesus die?** The good news is that Jesus died to take the punishment we deserve, giving his life as a ransom for many. This opened up the way for us into God's presence (Mark 15:37-38).

- **Why did Jesus rise?** The good news is that Jesus is alive, having conquered death. He offers forgiveness and life after death to all who will trust him (Mark 16:6-7).

- **How can God accept us?** The good news is that what is impossible for us is possible with God (Mark 10:26-27). We can't earn our acceptance with God – it is an undeserved gift. He freely offers it to us if we come humbly, like little children, and follow Jesus (Mark 10:15).

Note: Hopefully your group will be able to answer these questions from the things they have learned during the course. However, if they are struggling with a question, do point them to the verses given above.

> **3. "Repent and believe the good news!" (Mark 1:15)**
> To *repent* literally means to turn back in the opposite direction to the one you were travelling in.
> And to *believe the good news* means to act upon it, to build your life upon it.
> What would that mean for you?

This is designed to provoke reflection and application of the points made in questions 1 and 2. You may want to further explain "repent" as "to turn away from going your own way, and turn towards God and start going his way".

If the group members need prompting, you could give examples from your own life of turning back from misunderstandings about God and sin, repenting of sin and trusting in Christ.

LISTEN

(Page 60 in the group member's Handbook) *Encourage the group to make notes and list questions they may have as they listen to the Bible talk or watch the DVD. There is space in the Handbook to make notes.*

"If anyone would come after me, he must deny himself and take up his cross and follow me." (Mark 8:34)

- The disciples saw Jesus' power and authority – but still asked: "Who is this?"

- Jesus healed a blind man gradually.

- The gradual healing of the man's sight reflects the gradual growth of the disciples' understanding.

- Peter sees that Jesus is the Christ, God's only chosen King.

- But the disciples' "sight" is not fully healed. Although they see who Jesus is, they don't yet see why he has come or what it means to follow him.

- Following Jesus means denying self, and taking up our cross.

- If we want to save our lives, we must entrust them to Jesus.

- A true follower of Christ is someone who clearly sees what it will cost to follow him – but does it joyfully anyway, knowing that Jesus is worth infinitely more.

- What do you see when you look at:

    - Jesus' **identity**? (Is he just a good man, or is he the Christ, the Son of God?)

    - Jesus' **mission**? (Is his death a tragic waste, or is it a rescue – a "ransom for many"?)

    - Jesus' **call**? (Is it a way of losing your life, or a way of gaining it?)

DISCUSS

(Page 61 in the group member's Handbook) *Ask your group if there was anything that stood out or particularly struck them from the talk/DVD. This will help them to respond specifically to what they have just heard, before moving on to the group discussion questions.*

"What good is it for a man to gain the whole world, yet forfeit his soul?" (Mark 8:36) How would you answer that question?

This question is designed to reveal the ultimate value of the human soul, and the need to be forgiven and put right with God by trusting in Christ.

How might you be ashamed of Jesus and his words (Mark 8:38)?

The question is designed to help the group reflect on the reality of Jesus' call to discipleship. Answers might include:

- Embarrassment in front of friends, family and colleagues if they discovered you were a Christian.

- Unwillingness to tell others the good news about Jesus because of how they might react.

- Fear of being treated as intolerant, homophobic, anti-Muslim etc if you stand up for what Jesus said about these and other "sensitive" areas.

How would you score the following statements? (0 = completely unconvinced, 10 = very sure)
  Jesus is the Christ, the Son of God
  Jesus came to rescue me from my sin
  Following Jesus means denying myself and putting Jesus first, whatever the cost.

The group member's Handbook includes three horizontal lines representing *identity*, *mission* and *call*. Ask the group members to put a cross on each line to score themselves from 0 to 10, using the questions above to help them. Alternatively, if they prefer, they can just write down a number for each answer.

The scores group members give themselves will help you to get a feel for where they each are in their understanding and response to the gospel message.

WHAT NOW?

🔲 *Give a brief conclusion. If you have more than one discussion group, this is best given by the course leader or speaker to everyone together. (The wording below is intended only as a general guide.)*

As we draw the course to a close the natural question is: *What do we do now?* Although we have gone through the course as a group, we must respond personally to the good news. We are not here to put pressure on people to make commitments they are not ready to make. That would be the opposite of Jesus' example that we have seen in Mark 8. Nevertheless, the good news does demand a response from us individually.

Let's close with that phrase of Jesus from the opening chapter of Mark.

> *"'The time has come,' he said. 'The kingdom of God is near. Repent and believe the good news!'"* Mark 1:15

This is a call to action. The time has come. *(Let the group members feel the weight of this.)*

It is not enough to *know* who Jesus is, why he came and what it means to follow him. We have to *act* on what we have come to understand – we have to respond to this good news.

There are three aspects to the command of Jesus here.

1. The kingdom of God is near

We must understand that Jesus comes to us as a conquering King. His kingdom is near. Mark has shown us the power and authority Jesus has over every other power. We have also seen that by nature we rebel against the rule of God.

How will you respond to God's King? Will you continue to resist him? Or will you gladly become his subject?

2. Repent

To live with Jesus as King involves repentance. To repent means to turn back in the opposite direction to the one you were travelling in – to turn back to God from sin. It doesn't mean we think we can live perfectly from now on – we can't. But it does mean that we face up to our personal rebellion against God and confess it to him.

3. Believe the good news

To believe the good news means we gladly accept and live by the fact that Jesus died for sin and rose from the dead to rescue us from it. The good news is that rebels who turn back to God by trusting in what Jesus has done for them are welcome in his kingdom for ever. We know our sin no longer separates us from God.

> "'The time has come,' he said. 'The kingdom of God is near. Repent and believe the good news!'" Mark 1:15

How will you respond?

📖 *Note to leaders:*

Give the group an opportunity to respond. Understandably, some may not want to talk openly so offer to speak privately with people if they'd prefer.

There are broadly speaking three possible responses guests could make at the end of the course:

For those who are not ready to follow Jesus, but would still like to learn more, you might suggest: coming to church with you, meeting with you for one-to-one Bible study, doing *Christianity Explored* another time, or reading a good Christian book that addresses questions they may have. See "After the course" on page 57 for help in following up group members. You can find suggestions for recommended books from **www.ceministries.org**

For those who do not want to follow Jesus, and show no interest in taking things further: let them know how much you've valued getting to know them, and offer to meet up for a coffee in a few weeks' time if they'd like.

For those who have heard the call to "repent and believe", and want to begin following Jesus: help them understand what it means to "repent and believe".

Only God, by his Holy Spirit, can enable a person to repent and believe. "Repent" means to turn around from the direction we're currently headed in, and turn back to God. It means we start living life to please him, rather than continuing to rebel against him. "Believe" means believing that Jesus is who he says he is, and putting our trust in him as a result. It means being *for* what he is *for*, and *against* what he is *against*. As Jesus himself said: "If you love me, you will obey what I command" (John 14:15).

So to repent and believe is something that we do decisively at a moment in time, but it is not just a moment to look back on, it is a new way of life from now on. Help your group member to see what repentance and belief will look like:

- **A new attitude to God.** A follower of Jesus is deeply thankful to God, longs to know him better, love him better and be increasingly amazed by him. This longing is nurtured by reading his word, the Bible, and praying to him.

  Encourage your group member by offering to read the Bible one-to-one with them, and suggesting some daily Bible-reading notes. A follow-up course like *Discipleship Explored* is also a great way for a new believer to get started. (See **www.ceministries.org** for information about *Discipleship Explored*.)

  Rather than asking someone to read or repeat a prayer, encourage them to pray to God about what they've discovered on the course, thanking him for Jesus and what he means to them. Assure them that they can speak freely in their own words, because God looks into our hearts and understands our real longings – even if our words are hesitant and uncertain.

- **A new attitude to ourselves.** A follower of Jesus longs to please him by rejecting sin, and living for Jesus instead. There will be areas of our lives which we know (or will come to see) are not pleasing to him. To repent and believe means that we turn away from those ways of living, and try to live life in the way God intends. This is the life Jesus described as "life to the full" (John 10:10).

- **A new attitude to God's people.** A follower of Christ longs to be with others who follow Christ, as they encourage and support one another in the church family. As Jesus said: "Love one another. As I have loved you, so you must love one another. By this all men will know that you are my disciples, if you love one another" (John 13:34-35).

  "Baptism" is a way of identifying with Christ and his people, so encourage them to speak to their pastor or minister about being baptized.

  Offer to meet your group member at church on Sunday, and help them to establish a pattern of attending each week. Encourage them to join a small group, and to use whatever skills they have in serving their brothers and sisters in Christ.

If someone says they have repented and believed the good news, encourage them to think and behave as a believer, and to rejoice as a member of God's kingdom.

CONCLUSION

◉ *Explain to the group that you want to know what they thought of Christianity Explored, so that you can do it better next time. Ask them to fill out the Feedback form (see pages 57-58). Assure them that their forms will be treated with strict confidence, and not shown to anyone else.*

◉ *As you are saying goodbye to the group, however they have responded, let them know how much you've appreciated their company on the course. And do continue to pray for all your group members once the course has ended.*

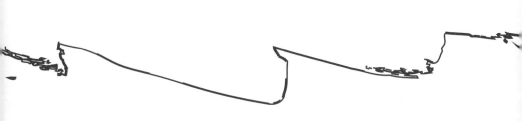

Day Away

DAY AWAY

Before you go

People need to have a clear understanding of what the Christian life entails before committing to it. They need time to reflect on what they have heard about the *identity*, *mission* and *call* of Jesus – and to understand the implications if they do or don't respond to his call and follow him.

With that in mind, the day away has been placed before Session 7 – the final session – when group members are invited to "repent and believe" (Mark 1:15).

- In Session 4, let guests know that there will be a day away and hand out invitations. Give a brief idea of what will happen, and ask them to block out the time in their calendars. (If your group members lead particularly busy lives, you may need to do this sooner.)

- In Sessions 5 and 6, hand out schedules for the day. (Most people like to have information about what is planned before they decide to come.) If you will be meeting in a different venue from usual, make sure everyone knows how to get there, and offer help with transport if needed.

- Arrange catering for the day away, including any special dietary requirements.

- Decide whether or not you need to make a small charge to cover the cost of the food. If you do, make this clear on the invitations.

- Check whether you are covered by the insurance for your church or organisation. If not, arrange separate insurance cover.

- If you will be away from your usual venue, check what the facilities will be for projecting PowerPoint slides, showing DVDs or other audio-visual needs. Arrange for spare Bibles or Mark's Gospels to be available for anyone who has forgotten theirs.

- Leaders will need to encourage guests to sign up for the weekend or day away.

- It is important for leaders to attend if group members in their care have signed up.

- Ensure that your prayer team has been notified and that they are praying ahead. Give them a copy of the schedule for the day.

- During the day away, there should be no singing, praying or anything that could make guests feel unduly pressured or uncomfortable.

- The day away allows plenty of time for leaders to continue to build trusting relationships with guests. Use the free time for activities that will facilitate this (for example, walks in the country, playing a team sport, visiting local attractions or making something together).

- Leaders' testimonies are also important, because they give guests an insight into the practicalities of Christian living. Choose a leader to present his or her testimony and help them to prepare what they will say. (Practical advice on preparing testimonies can also be found in Section 1 on page 40). Testimonies can be presented at any point during the day away.

- *List those you will ask to give their testimony.*

Example day away invitation

Feel like escaping for the day?

Why not join us for a relaxing day of food, conversation and a few more short DVDs? It'll be a chance to enjoy some good company and teaching in an unhurried atmosphere.

Lunch (and popcorn!) will be provided.

Time: **10 a.m. until 6.30 p.m.**

Place: **Community Hall, Main Street**

Cost: **Free**

Just complete the slip below if you would like to come, then give it to your leader.

....

NAME: _____

TELEPHONE: _____

ADDRESS: _____

_____

Any special dietary requirements? _____

I can/cannot offer transport to _____ people.

I require transport ☐ Yes   ☐ No

An editable version of this invitation is available from **www.ceministries.org**

Example day away schedule

Arrive	10:00 a.m.
Welcome and coffee	10:30 a.m.
1: THE SOWER: "Listen carefully" **followed by group discussion**	11:00 a.m.
Coffee	12:00 p.m.
2: JAMES AND JOHN: "Ask humbly" **followed by group discussion**	12:30 p.m.
Lunch	1:30 p.m.
Free time	2:30 p.m.
"Real lives" **Meet some members of the church family**	4:30 p.m.
Coffee	5:00 p.m.
3: HEROD: "Choose wisely" **followed by group discussion**	5:30 p.m.
Leave	6:30 p.m.

An editable version of this schedule is available from **www.ceministries.org**

DAY AWAY

Introduction

▣ *Welcome the group and thank them for coming. Give out copies of the schedule so that people know what to expect, and when the refreshment breaks will be. If you are not meeting in your usual venue, let people know where refreshments and lunch will be served, and the location of the toilets.*

▣ *Deliver the introduction using the notes below. These notes can also be downloaded from **www.ceministries.org** to enable you to adapt them for your group.*

Welcome to our day away together. We are delighted you have carved out the time to join us. I just want to say a word about the purpose and programme for the day.

PURPOSE

There are a couple of times in Mark where Jesus takes the disciples away from the normal demands of their busy lives. He wanted to give them an opportunity to reflect on what he taught. That, in a nutshell, is the purpose of today. Mark has introduced us to the remarkable person and mission of Jesus. Today is an opportunity to get some time away; to relax and enjoy each other's company. But above all it is a time to think through the implications of what we have heard, and to discuss these things.

PROGRAMME (add your own timings)

Session 1: The Sower – Listen carefully (Mark 4:1-9; 13-20)

We will look at one of Jesus' stories – often called "The parable of the sower". This story will remind us of the power of the gospel message – power to change our lives – and the responsibility we have to hear and receive it.

There will be a tea/coffee break at _____

Session 2: James and John – Ask humbly (Mark 10:35-52)

Twice in this section of Mark Jesus asks: "What do you want me to do for you?" We will investigate what we think we most need in life.

We will have lunch together at _____

We then have some free time after lunch. (Let people know the options for how they can spend the free time.)

"Real lives"

Later in the afternoon we have some friends from the church coming to meet you, and to tell you a little of their journey to faith in Jesus.

There will be a tea/coffee break at _____

Session 3: Herod – Choose wisely (Mark 6:17-29)

In our final session we will look at a king who liked to listen to a preacher. But this king chose not to act on what the preacher said, and found himself powerless over the circumstances that developed.

PS

One of those times when Jesus took the disciples away for some teaching and thinking time is recorded in Mark 9:30-32. We are told that, unfortunately, they did not understand what Jesus meant and were afraid to ask him about it. Please don't follow their example. As always, we would love to hear your thoughts and questions as we go through the day.

▣ *At the end of this introduction move straight on to Session 1: The sower.*

1: THE SOWER

Listen carefully

EXPLORE

- *Ask the group members to turn to the day away section on page 49 of the Handbook.*

- *Ask everyone to open their Mark's Gospels or Bibles at Mark 4. One of the leaders should read Mark 4:1-9 and 13-20.*

- *Work through the questions below to help the group explore the passage.*

1. A parable is a story with a deeper, sometimes hidden, meaning. What does each part of this parable represent? (See Mark 4:13-20.)

The farmer represents: those who "sow the word" (Mark 4:14) ie: those who tell people the gospel message, the good news about Jesus Christ.

The seed is: "the word" (Mark 4:14) ie: the word of God, the Bible's message about Jesus (his identity, mission and call).

The path is like people who: hear the gospel message, but "Satan comes and takes away the word" (Mark 4:15) ie: they hear about Jesus but quickly forget what they have heard.

The rocky soil is like those who: are full of joy at what they hear, but "last only a short time" (Mark 4:16-17) ie: they respond well at first but fall away when trouble comes as a result of following Jesus.

What are the thorns in real life? The thorns are "the worries of this life, the deceitfulness of wealth and the desires for other things" (Mark 4:19). Ask your group what these things might be for them.

How would you recognize those who are good soil? Those who are good soil hear the gospel message, accept it and continue to be transformed by it, and live fruitful lives for God.

LISTEN

▣ *(Page 50 in the group member's Handbook)* *Encourage the group to make notes and list questions they may have as they listen to the Bible talk or watch the DVD. There is space in the Handbook to make notes.*

"Then Jesus said, 'He who has ears to hear, let him hear.' "
(Mark 4:9)

▣ The good news about Jesus will only change your life if you hear it properly.

▣ The parable explains four different responses to the good news.

1. Satan is like a thief who wants to take the gospel message from you.

2. Some people give up on Jesus rather than put up with the cost of following him.

3. Some let their desire for other things become stronger than their desire for Jesus.

4. Some understand that Jesus is the greatest treasure in the world.

▣ The gospel message has the power to break through any human heart, if we will listen and act on what we hear.

DISCUSS

📖 (Page 51 in the group member's Handbook) Ask your group if there was anything that stood out or particularly struck them from the talk/DVD. This will help them to respond specifically to what they have just heard, before moving on to the group discussion questions.

> **As you look back over the course, do you think some of the word has been taken from you?**

If any of the group says "yes", ask them to explain what they mean. For example, someone may have missed several sessions, or been so busy that they haven't thought about what they've heard or done any of the "Follow up" reading at home.

Group members need to be aware that Satan wants to take the gospel message from them – but do reassure them that the devil does not have the final say. Jesus has beaten Satan by his death on the cross. Encourage group members to respond properly to the things they have heard, rather than worrying about the bits they've missed.

Note: If a guest has missed a large part of the course, it may be worth encouraging them to do the course again, or offering the option of someone working through the material with them individually.

> **Which type of soil would you say best describes you?**

This question will help group members consider what their own response has been so far to the good news about Jesus. They will be challenged further about their response in the final section of the day away.

2: JAMES AND JOHN

Ask humbly

■ Ask the guests to turn to page 52 of the Handbook.

■ Explain that Sessions 2 and 3 of the day away do not include an "Explore" Bible study. Instead, we will go straight in to the talk/DVD.

LISTEN

■ Encourage the group to make notes and list questions they may have as they listen to the Bible talk or watch the DVD. There is space in the Handbook to make notes.

"What do you want me to do for you?" (Mark 10:36)

▣ If God said: "What do you want me to do for you?", what would you ask for?

▣ James and John wanted power and prestige but Jesus offers something far more valuable – himself.

▣ Following Jesus is about service, not status.

▣ Contentment, satisfaction and fulfilment don't come from status-seeking, or anything else – they come from God.

▣ We make these things more important than God. The Bible calls this idolatry – turning something God has created into a substitute for God.

▣ Bartimaeus called Jesus "Son of David" and asked for mercy. He received it, and followed Jesus.

▣ What do you want Jesus to do for you?

DISCUSS

(Page 53 in the group member's Handbook) *Ask your group if there was anything that stood out or particularly struck them from the talk/DVD. This will help them to respond specifically to what they have just heard, before moving on to the group discussion questions.*

Who do you identify with most and why?
James and John? Or Bartimaeus?

This question will help your group to apply the teaching from the talk/DVD to their own situation. If anyone says they don't identify with either James and John or with Bartimaeus, ask them to explain why.

What do you want Jesus to do for you?

This question is a very personal challenge for each member of the group. Encourage them to share their answers, but don't force anyone to say something if they don't want to. For some, their answer may be that they don't know what they want Jesus to do for them. If so, encourage them to keep coming to the rest of the course, and, if possible, let them know that there will be further opportunities to keep exploring the message of Christianity.

The healing of Bartimaeus may have raised the issue of healing in some people's minds, in which case their answer might be that they want healing for themselves or someone else. See "Why does God allow suffering?" in the appendix on page 248 for some help in answering this question.

"Real lives"

The day away provides an opportunity for others from your church or organisation to serve those who have been doing the *Christianity Explored* course. For example, people who can't be regular leaders may be able to give some time to setting up the venue, serving refreshments or cooking lunch. This will give guests an opportunity to meet some other members of the church family.

One or more of these people may also be suitable to give their testimonies during the "Real lives" session in the afternoon.

TESTIMONIES

Choose two or three people from the church who, ideally, represent the age and gender profile of the *Christianity Explored* group. Invite them to have lunch with the group and introduce them. The most important factor in selecting these people is their ability to speak plainly and helpfully about their journey to faith in Christ and their experience of Christian living.

In the afternoon (after lunch or free time, depending on your programme) ask them to give a realistic testimony, either directly or by interview. See page 40 for help in preparing a testimony.

Ask them to talk about:

- how they came to trust in Christ

- the joys and struggles of Christian discipleship

- the support they have found in the local church (eg: small groups, one-to-one Bible reading, book and media stall etc)

- God speaking to them as they read the Bible and hear it taught

Check that those giving testimonies are happy to be asked questions, and encourage the *Christianity Explored* group to chat to them during the coffee break.

3: HEROD

Choose wisely

LISTEN

(Page 54 in the group member's Handbook) Encourage the group to make notes and list questions they may have as they listen to the Bible talk or watch the DVD. There is space in the Handbook to make notes.

"The king was greatly distressed, but because of his oaths and his dinner guests, he did not want to refuse her." (Mark 6:26)

- We are the choices we have made.

- King Herod had John the Baptist put in prison.

- He liked to listen to John, but would not repent.

- Herod didn't act on what John said about Herodias. So in the end he felt forced to do something he didn't want to do – and had John killed.

- If we listen to Jesus, and take his words seriously, our family or friends may reject us. But there is a loving family of fellow believers who will support and encourage us.

- Though following Jesus will bring persecutions of one kind or another, Jesus promises that with them will come extraordinary blessings and joy.

- Ignoring Jesus' call to repent and believe may give us the approval of other people – but it will eventually earn us the rejection of Jesus.

DISCUSS

■ *(Page 55 in the group member's Handbook) Ask your group if there was anything that stood out or particularly struck them from the talk/DVD. This will help them to respond specifically to what they have just heard, before moving on to the group discussion questions.*

> **How do you think Herod felt about killing John the Baptist? (See Mark 6:20, 26, and then Mark 6:16.)**

Mark 6:20 – Herod knew that John was "righteous and holy", and did not deserve the treatment he received, so he may have felt guilty. He liked to listen to John, so may have been sorry to lose that opportunity.

Mark 6:26 – Herod was distressed by the demand for John's head, but didn't want to refuse in front of his dinner guests. He didn't want to have John killed, but was caught in a trap of his own making. He may have felt he didn't have a choice – but that's not true! He could (and should) have refused the girl's request.

Mark 6:16 suggests that Herod was still thinking about John. Herod may have felt guilty for what he'd done, and perhaps worried that he was going to have to meet the man he had killed.

> **Mark tells us that "the opportune time came" (Mark 6:21). What opportunity did Herodias take? (See Mark 6:19, 24.)**

Herodias had wanted to kill John the Baptist for some time (Mark 6:19), but couldn't because Herod was protecting him. Herod's foolish oath to her daughter gave Herodias the opportunity to have John "immediately" killed (Mark 6:27).

> **What opportunity did Herod miss, and why?**

Herod missed the opportunity to repent: that is, to turn from what he knew was wrong, and turn back to God. He liked to listen to John, who he knew to be "a righteous and holy man" (Mark 6:20). He had heard John's clear message that his marriage to his brother's wife, Herodias, was wrong (Mark 6:18) – but had refused to repent. At the banquet Herod had the opportunity to save John's life and repent of his foolish oath to the daughter of Herodias. But he wasn't willing to do this in front of his dinner guests, so he gave the order for John's execution.

What kind of soil is Herod? (See Mark 4:15-20.)

Herod is the soil filled with thorns (Mark 4:18-19). He heard the word of God, taught clearly by John the Baptist, but other things choked it and made it unfruitful.

An old saying says: "We are the choices we have made." How was that true for Herod?

Herod had chosen to take his brother's wife and marry her. He refused to repent when John told him he was wrong. His wrong relationship with Herodias, and her hatred of John, led to Herod agreeing to John's execution. He had the opportunity to listen to God's word as spoken by John, but didn't take it. Later on, when Herod met Jesus, the opportunity had gone and Jesus didn't answer any of Herod's questions (Luke 23:9).

What choices will you make about the things you have heard during *Christianity Explored*?

This question is designed to challenge each group member personally about their own choices, and the implications of those.

Supplementary question:

If you have time left over at the end of this discussion, ask the following:

Mark tells us that, "When Herod heard John, he was greatly puzzled; yet he liked to listen to him" (Mark 6:20). Having heard the good news about Jesus during *Christianity Explored*, did you enjoy listening and discussing? Are you puzzled by anything?

If there are any questions still unanswered from the "If you could ask God one question…" discussion in Session 1, answer them here.

At the end of this session move straight on to the conclusion overleaf.

DAY AWAY

Conclusion

*Deliver the conclusion using the notes below. These notes can also be downloaded from **www.ceministries.org** to enable you to adapt them for your group.*

As we draw the day to a close let me thank you once again for joining us. I hope you have enjoyed the opportunity to think through the implications of the good news about Jesus.

I hope you can see that to know Jesus and receive all the wonderful gifts of grace he gives – rescue, forgiveness, the Holy Spirit – we have to come to him empty handed. We can't buy or earn these things, and we can't share him with the "desires for other things" that we read about in Session 1 today. Jesus is the ultimate treasure in the universe, and in the end knowing him is all that matters.

We look forward to seeing you again on _____ at _____ for Session 7, our final time on this course. We will be looking at Mark 8, what it means to follow Jesus.

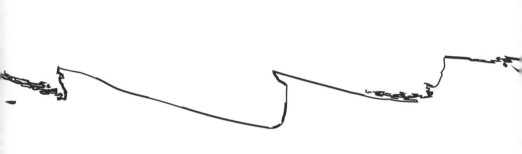

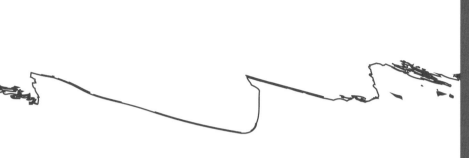

1: GOOD NEWS

What are we doing here?

- *Deliver Talk 1 using the notes below. The notes for this talk can also be downloaded from **www.ceministries.org** to enable you to adapt them for your group and add your own illustrations. Alternatively you could show Episode 1 (Good News) from the Christianity Explored DVD if this would be appropriate for your group.*

- *There is a bulleted talk outline on page 6 of the group member's Handbook. Encourage people to write notes next to this outline as they listen to the talk.*

Aim

- To welcome people to the course.

- To recognize and challenge guests' preconceptions about Christianity.

- To show that Christianity is "good news" about Jesus Christ (Mark 1:1).

- To challenge the group to discover what that good news is by making time to come to this course and to reading Mark's Gospel.

Introduction

What's the most beautiful sight you've ever seen?

For me it was probably... (*Give a personal story describing a staggering sight of natural beauty.*)

What would it be for you?

And when you saw what you saw, I wonder if you asked yourself the same questions I did... what kind of power could have produced something so achingly beautiful that it reduces a human being to sheer, wordless wonder?

We live in an amazing world.

Millions of millions of miles above us, apparently, there are at least 100 billion stars. And those are just the ones in our own Milky Way galaxy. The better our technology gets, the more galaxies we see, but currently, scientists estimate there are at least 100 billion galaxies in the universe.

And it's not just the larger things in life that are truly remarkable – it's the smaller things too.

Did you know there are 75 thousand miles of blood vessels crammed inside us and there are at least 50 trillion cells. These are mind-blowing statistics! If the DNA from a single human cell were stretched out, it would measure about six feet in length.

So if the entire DNA contained within the cells of a single human being was stretched out and laid end to end, it would reach all the way to the moon. And back again. Eight thousand times.

Surely the sheer wonder of life should raise huge questions for us…

Does the mindlessness of blind chance explain this amazing world?

How did life begin, without life to create it in the first place?

And even if I *do* decide it all happened completely by chance, why is there anything here at all? Why is there something… and not nothing?

The Bible unashamedly says that all this natural beauty and amazing intricacy is meant to point us towards God, the one who created the extraordinary scale and complexity of the universe we live in, and the bodies we inhabit.

But this is the point at which many people switch off. They may have caught something of the marvel of creation, but Christianity leaves them cold.

Someone calculated that if you took all the people who sleep through church services on a Sunday, and laid them end-to-end on the floor… they would be a lot more comfortable!

Many people have cut the connection between life in all its wonder and the Christian faith. So it's important to say at the beginning of *Christianity Explored* that we are well aware that many people find Christianity incredibly dull, and entirely irrelevant.

You might be looking at Mark's book and asking yourself: "What's the point of reading something written 2000 years ago and 2000 miles away?" – especially if, as well as thinking it is boring and irrelevant, you are also pretty sure that the contents of the Bible are untrue.

The *Christianity Explored* course is designed by people who once felt that way too. The course exists to clear away all the misconceptions about Christianity so that you can examine the facts for yourself.

That's why we begin with the very first sentence of Mark. It says this:

"The beginning of the gospel about Jesus Christ..." (Mark 1:1).

If you think Christianity is all about churches, and rules – leaving your brain at the door and then having all your fun spoiled – you have been misled.

That's not what it's about. The first sentence of Mark's Gospel says that Christianity is about **Christ**, Jesus Christ.

The word "Christ" there isn't a surname; it is a title, like President or Prime Minister. And it means "God's only chosen King". It was a dangerous word for Mark to use at a time when the Roman Emperor was worshipped as though he was a god.

To speak of *Jesus* as God's only true representative on earth was the kind of thing that got you thrown into the Coliseum to be torn apart by wild animals.

Actually, Mark's claim that Jesus is the Christ, God's only chosen King, is just as controversial today. I wonder what you make of it?

Mark says his book is *"The beginning of the **gospel** about Jesus Christ"*. The word "gospel" means "good news."

I don't know how you answered the question about the best news you have ever heard, but when Mark uses the phrase good news, he is speaking about news that is so good, it is life-changing. It's like the news that war is over and you are on the winning side.

So Mark 1:1 tells us that the gospel – the exceptionally good news – is all about Jesus Christ.

I have to be honest and say that I understand those who find the Christian faith useless, meaningless, unappealing or unbelievable. But the problem is that, often, what they have written off is not the real thing.

I would be bored by some of the experiences on offer that go under the name of Christianity.

💬 *Include a personal example here – either of a boring or negative experience of Christianity you once had, or the experience of someone you know.*

You may have had similar bad experiences of religion. If so, I hope you will stick around to see how un-religious Jesus is. You may well be surprised by the Jesus you encounter.

Christianity is about Christ

From this verse we know what Mark is **not** about. It doesn't say the beginning of the gospel about being religious, keeping rules and being miserable. No, it says the beginning of the gospel about Jesus Christ.

It doesn't say the beginning of the gospel about "throwing your brain out of the window". You don't have to suspend your mental faculties to believe in Jesus – because he is a real person who lived and walked and talked in human history. He is someone who can be investigated.

This is not the beginning of the gospel about "old, ornate buildings, dusty history and strange ways of dressing and speaking".

No, it's about Jesus Christ. And when we look at him, the guessing games about God stop. The God of the Bible is not someone we dreamed up! We aren't going to bore you with our theories about God. No, God has revealed himself to us. God has shown us what he is like by sending his Son, Jesus Christ.

Mark 1:1 is an invitation to read on and encounter the best news a person could ever hear. If, at the moment, you don't think that Christianity is the best and most thrilling news you have ever heard, can I say again that you must have misunderstood it. And there are many who have done so.

Now that is a bold statement for me to make, but let me reassure you that Christianity Explored isn't designed to indoctrinate people. We're running this course to give you an opportunity to see the facts for yourself.

Will you test Mark's claim?

The question is: Will you take the time to test Mark's claim? Will you see for yourself if he is telling you the best news ever?

The following true illustration shows how easily people can miss out on something that's great. If you have a personal illustration, or one that is local to your area or culture, do use that instead.

I'm sure you've had the experience of walking through (give the name of your town's main street) and being offered a leaflet which you refuse – or take and then ignore – because you don't think it'll do you any good.

Well, the British newspaper, the Evening Standard, once conducted an experiment. They got a man to stand outside Oxford Circus station in central London handing out leaflets. On the leaflet was the free offer of £5 for just bringing the leaflet back to the man.

Hordes of people passed him, and in three hours only eleven came back for their £5. People assumed they knew what he was handing out and that it would do them no good – so they didn't bother to take it or read it.

My plea is that you don't make the same mistake with the Bible. If you want to find out what God is like, and how you're supposed to relate to him, then this (*hold up a Bible or Mark's Gospel*) is all you need.

On this course we will discover from Mark's Gospel who Jesus is, why he came into the world, and what it means to follow him. This is big news, and it is great news.

📄 *You could use this illustration:*

It is rather like admiring a car that is for sale, and the person who is selling it hands you the key and says you can test drive it for a few weeks – to put it through its paces, see how it works, and discover if it is a car you would like to own.

On *Christianity Explored* we are saying: "Here is Mark's Gospel – here is the ignition key to Christianity. Take it for a test drive for seven weeks. Ask any questions you like, put the Christian world-view through its paces, see how it works, and discover if it makes sense of life in a way that nothing else does."

Where Mark begins

📄 *If you have already given the group Bibles or copies of Mark's Gospel, ask them to turn to Mark chapter 1. Give them the page number so that no one need feel embarrassed about trying to find it.*

Let me put the key in your hand as I introduce you to the unfolding drama of Mark's Gospel...

The opening section of Mark's Gospel prepares us for an exceptional encounter. In chapter 1, verses 2-3, Mark quotes from the Old Testament – the part of the Bible which covers the history of God's dealings with humanity from creation right through to the period before the coming of Jesus into the world.

👁 **Read Mark 1:2-3**

These words were written over 700 years before Jesus was born! The point Mark wants us to see is that the coming of Jesus into the world was not an afterthought on God's part. These verses show that this was always the plan. As Jesus came into the world and began his ministry, God's plan was being fulfilled precisely and with amazing accuracy.

Mark introduces us to John – often known as John the Baptist, because he baptized people in the Jordan River. John came to prepare the way for Jesus, as verse 4 shows.

👁 Read Mark 1:4

His was *"the voice of one calling in the desert"* that had been spoken about hundreds of years earlier. Then notice verses 7-8:

👁 Read Mark 1:7-8

Mark's sudden leap into the Old Testament shows that people had been waiting a very long time for the person God was going to send. It is the equivalent to waiting at the airport for a long-overdue flight to arrive.

📝 *If possible include a personal example of waiting a long time for a flight that you really want to arrive. Eg: because it is bringing a family member or friend you've not seen for several years.*

You have almost given up hope, and then the blank arrivals screen comes to life with an announcement of an expected arrival, in red; and then finally, in green, the word "landed" appears.

That's what Mark is telling us. God had promised to send a King. We have the Old Testament prophecies which point forward to the exact place and nature of his coming.

Mark shows us how John the Baptist came, quite suddenly, to say the arrival on earth of God's King was expected and imminent. And then verses 9-11 are the green "landed" sign.

What happens when God's King arrives

👁 Read Mark1:9-11

This is an astonishing start. We are told that heaven gets torn open; the Holy Spirit comes down on Jesus like a dove; and God the Father announces: *"You are my Son"*.

Clearly Jesus is the "more powerful" one of whom John spoke in verse 7.

I need to tell you that encountering God's promised King – Jesus – in Mark's Gospel takes us into a whole different realm. But I would encourage you to realize that exceptional events beyond human ability are bound to be part of the scene when God the Son steps into human flesh and comes to the world he has made.

If Jesus is just a human, then what we read is unbelievable. But if he is God in human flesh, then it should not surprise us when staggering things happen. Supernatural things.

The best news in the world

And don't miss the big point here. John the Baptist tells us in verse 8 that Jesus came to baptize people in the Holy Spirit. That means to bring ordinary people like us into the life-giving, life-changing power of God.

John's ministry had its limit – he baptized with water. Mark tells us that...

> *"The whole Judean countryside and all the people of Jerusalem went out to him"* (Mark 1:5).

The people flocked to John because if God was coming, they needed to be ready. They knew from their own experience that they were not the people they wanted to be, let alone the people God wanted them to be.

So John offered them baptism with water, as a sign of being washed clean, of being forgiven.

When the person was lowered into the water, it was a symbol of dying to their old way of living, and when they were lifted out of the water, it was a symbol of being raised to new life. But John knew that the Lord himself would offer them – and us – so much more.

> *"I baptise you with water, but he will baptise you with the Holy Spirit"* (Mark 1:8).

What John is saying is absolutely stunning. He is claiming that Jesus Christ will not only offer complete forgiveness to all those who put their trust in him. He will also fill those people with God's Holy Spirit, who will radically transform their lives.

To those who know they are not the people they want to be, let alone the people God wants them to be, this is the best, the most remarkable news in the world.

And let me reassure you that if all this seems a bit too much for Session 1, in his first chapter Mark is giving us a glimpse of the end of the process, God's Spirit coming to live in us.

It is as though he meets us at the factory gates where the finished product leaves. He shows us the end of the process. But he will take us along the assembly line and explain step by step who Jesus is, how much we need him and how we can have a full and joyful relationship with him.

And that is exactly what *Christianity Explored* is all about. At the heart of the gospel message is the astonishing truth that God has not remained distant but has come to us in the person of Jesus Christ.

Christianity is Christ. The real Jesus is worth meeting. That's why Christianity is worth exploring.

So, how do you feel about taking a seven-week test drive?

2: IDENTITY
Who is Jesus?

🔅 *Deliver Talk 2 using the notes below. The notes for this talk can also be downloaded from www.ceministries.org to enable you to adapt them for your group and add your own illustrations. Alternatively you could show Episode 2 (Identity) from the Christianity Explored DVD if this would be appropriate for your group.*

🔅 *There is a bulleted talk outline on page 13 of the group member's Handbook. Encourage people to write notes next to this outline as they listen to the talk.*

Aim

▪ To help the group see the evidence for the unique identity of Jesus.

▪ To show that Jesus has the power and authority of God.

▪ To challenge group members to consider the implications of this for their own lives.

Introduction

🔅 *Start with an illustration about how you have mistaken the identity of someone and it led to you treating them wrongly or ignoring them. If you do not have a story of your own, then use this true illustration:*

Have you ever completely missed who someone is... until it's too late? The creator of Christianity Explored, *Rico Tice*, was once invited to a lunch. As he waited outside the room, he found himself opposite a young man who looked vaguely familiar. For five minutes neither said a word, although the young man looked as if he expected Rico to speak to him. But Rico didn't know who he was, so said nothing. It was only as the young man left that Rico discovered his identity – Prince William, the future king of England.

Rico stood opposite Prince William for five minutes and didn't say a word. Because he didn't recognize him, he just saw a young man. He didn't see the future king, so he didn't take the opportunity to relate to him.

If we get someone's identity wrong, we'll relate to them in the wrong way. This week on *Christianity Explored* we'll look at what Mark's Gospel tells us about the identity of Jesus, and why Mark is convinced that Jesus is God's only chosen King. And it's important for us to get *this* King's identity right – otherwise we'll relate to him in the wrong way, or even ignore him completely.

Last week we saw that Mark starts his book with the words:

"The beginning of the gospel about Jesus Christ" (Mark 1:1).

Mark is saying that the message about Jesus is "good news" about the "Christ", God's only chosen King. That's quite a claim, so Mark backs it up in the first few chapters of his book. He piles up the evidence for who Jesus is.

We're going to look at five ways that Mark reveals Jesus' identity. Five examples of evidence that point to the conclusion that Jesus really is God's only chosen King.

1. Jesus had power and authority to teach

Mark tells us what happened when Jesus went to the Jewish place of worship, the synagogue:

👁 **Read Mark 1:21-22**

What set Jesus apart from the other teachers was the way he taught. The teachers of the law didn't come up with their own material. They only ever dealt in second-hand goods. They relied on the great teachers of the past, and just quoted them or gave their opinions of what those previous teachers had said.

But when Jesus came along and began to teach, the people were staggered. He taught things they'd never heard before. Mark says they were amazed at the personal authority with which he taught. They were hearing the word of God from the lips of the Son of God. And they were hearing it taught by someone who also lived it out. Listening to Jesus was like a light being switched on in the darkness.

That's why the people who heard him were "amazed" at his words, and asked each other: *"What is this? A new teaching – and with authority!"* (Mark 1:27).

Clearly, Jesus could teach – but did he also live out what he taught?

⚙ *You could include an illustration here of someone who says one thing but is then found to have done something completely different. For example a religious leader who has an affair, or a politician who steals government funds.*

We've all come across hypocrites who say one thing but do another. But Jesus wasn't like that. For example, he taught: *"Love your enemies and pray for those who persecute you"* (Matthew 5:44). Later, as he was being killed, he prayed for his executioners: *"Father, forgive them, for they do not know what they are doing"* (Luke 23:34). Now that is practising what you preach.

Here was a teacher who taught with power and authority. And who also lived out what he taught.

But Jesus wasn't just a teacher…

2. Jesus had power and authority over sickness

We've seen what happened when Jesus went *into* the synagogue and started to teach. Mark then tells us what happened when he *left*:

👁 **Read Mark 1:29-31**

Here's Jesus demonstrating absolute authority over sickness. Just a touch of his hand and the fever is cured. And this is not an isolated incident either.

The Bible has over thirty examples of Jesus healing people. And as a result: the deaf hear, the blind see, the lame walk, lepers are healed and restored.

Mark also tells us that Jesus cured people of spiritual suffering as well as physical suffering – releasing people from demonic oppression.

Now, the people of the time were obviously convinced that Jesus had extraordinary ability to heal. In Mark 1:45 we read that they *"came to him from everywhere"*.

No one, not even Jesus' enemies, doubted his power. His enemies wanted to discredit him, but couldn't deny the power he had. The evidence points to genuine, God-like healing ability.

These are astonishing miracles. But if Jesus Christ truly is the Son of God breaking into history, isn't this what you'd expect to see?

But Jesus wasn't just a teacher and healer…

3. Jesus had power and authority over nature

Let's think back to the story we talked about together – the story of Jesus calming the storm.

Isn't it amazing in this story to see the genuine humanity of Jesus? He is a real flesh-and-blood man. And here we see him in the stern of the boat, sleeping on a cushion. He is exhausted. But is he *just* a man?

The word translated "furious squall" can literally mean a whirlwind. The boat was nearly swamped. So the disciples woke Jesus and complained: *"Teacher, don't you care if we drown?"* (v 38).

Now several of the disciples were hardened fishermen. They'd sailed on Lake Galilee hundreds of times. If they think they're going to die, it must be serious.

Notice that they call him *"teacher"*. They know that Jesus speaks with authority. And they know he can heal the sick. So he has power... but does he care? That was their question: *"Teacher, don't you care if we drown?"*

What happens next is amazing:

> *"He got up, rebuked the wind and said to the waves, 'Quiet! Be still!' Then the wind died down and it was completely calm"* (Mark 4:39).

Do you see what we're being presented with here? Jesus not only has authority with people and over illness. In this instance, he speaks and the forces of nature – which have no ears to listen, and no brain to understand His command – respond instantly.

Jesus actually does two things here:

■ He stops the wind, which is the *cause* of the storm.

■ He calms the waves, which are the *result* of the storm.

■ *You could include a practical illustration here. For example, suggest this to the group:*

Next time you fill a bowl of water to wash some dishes, try rocking the bowl to make some waves. Then stop the rocking and watch what happens. Even though the bowl has stopped, the water doesn't. It continues to move from side to side for a long time. The same is true for waves on the sea.

Now normally it takes hours for the surface of the water to calm after a severe storm – because the swell has built up. But Jesus calms these waves instantly.

And after he flattened the sea, he said to his disciples: *"Why are you so afraid? Do you still have no faith?"*

What are they afraid of now? Are they afraid of the storm? It's calm.

> *"They were terrified and asked each other, 'Who is this? Even the wind and the waves obey him!'"* (Mark 4:41)

The disciples knew from their Old Testament that only Almighty God has the power to control the astonishing forces of nature. They would have sung psalms about this.

But it's one thing to grow up singing about a God who can calm the wind and waves. It's quite another to find yourself sitting in a boat with him – having rudely wakened him to ask him if he cares!

As they sit in the boat on the calmed sea, they begin to see what this miracle means. He gets tired like us and falls fast asleep. But unlike us, he has a word with the wind and waves, and they do as they are told. So the disciples ask: *"Who is this?"* The answer is obvious: who else can Jesus be but God in human flesh?

But, remarkable as that is, in the next chapter the disciples witness something even more astonishing…

4. Jesus had power and authority over death

👁 **Read Mark 5:21-22**

Jairus is a key man in the community, a figure of honour and respect. Yet he is flat on his face before Jesus.

We see why in verse 23:

> *"[Jairus] pleaded earnestly with him, 'My little daughter is dying. Please come and put your hands on her so that she will be healed and live.'"*

Here is a dad who has always provided for his little girl. He has always protected her and done all he can for her, but now he's desperate. Imagine the desperation and powerlessness you would feel if your own child was dying. That's the emotional intensity here.

💬 *Perhaps include a personal illustration here of your own experience of death and how it severs relationships with people we dearly love.*

So imagine Jairus' relief when Jesus agrees to go with him. He knows that Jesus has never failed to heal any illness.

But as they move off together, a lady comes to Jesus for help, and he stops to talk to her. This lady had been ill for as long as Jairus' daughter had been alive. But Jairus must have been beside himself with anxiety because of this delay.

Now pick up the story at verse 35:

👁 Read Mark 5:35

These men still call Jesus "teacher". They all know about his amazing teaching. Also that he could heal sickness and control the forces of nature. But they think there is a limit to the authority of Jesus. They think that limit has now been reached.

The men who bring the terrible news have seen the dead girl. So their view is: "Jesus may be a remarkable teacher. He may be able to make sick people well, which was what we hoped he would do for us. But she's no longer sick, she's dead. We don't need Jesus any more."

But listen to Jesus' extraordinary words in verse 36:

👁 Read Mark 5:36

Jesus ignores what they say! As Jesus hears that this girl has died, it apparently makes no difference to his plans. He ignores the "detail" of her death!

Let's have a look and see what happened next:

👁 Read Mark 5:37-40a

This is the laughter of scorn. Maybe, inwardly, you are laughing scornfully as well at the thought of Jesus being able to do these things. But if this is true, the implications are huge.

Jesus doesn't mean that the girl wasn't dead – she was. But he knew that it would be easier for him to bring her back to life than it is for you to wake a sleeping teenager.

Why? Because he is the Son of God, and has power and authority over death.

👁 Read Mark 5:40b-42

Isn't this a lovely intimate scene? Jesus has put the mockers outside. And Mum and Dad watch as he takes their daughter's hand. *"Talitha koum!"* – which means: "Little girl, I say to you, get up!". These were the words her father would have used every morning to wake her up.

And her eyes open. She gets up! And Jesus says: "Get her something to eat". No wonder they were *"completely astonished"*. Wouldn't you be?

Now, if this is a man who has power over death, surely it would be madness to ignore him – to say: "I'm just not interested in this" or "This is boring" or "Well that's fine for you to believe".

One day you and I are going to die. After the evidence we've just seen, the question we must ask ourselves is this: Can I trust Jesus with my own death?

But I have to say that *"Quiet! Be still!"* and *"Little girl … get up"* are not the most outrageous things Jesus says in Mark. For that we have to go back to chapter 2.

5. Jesus had power and authority to forgive sin

👁 **Read Mark 2:1-12**

I've had (*or* seen) some amazing interruptions when I have (*or* someone has) been speaking to groups.

▣ *Give an illustration of an interruption you've had while speaking to a group, or have seen happen to another speaker.*

But this interruption just beats everything. The roof gets ripped up. Pieces fall onto the crowd below. Then a shaft of daylight. Then it goes dark again as the stretcher is lowered and this poor man comes down with it.

And then we have the first words Jesus says to the man: *"Son, your sins are for-given".*

Why would Jesus say this? The obvious issue for this man is his paralysis. You can imagine him saying: "I'm sorry Jesus, it's not my sins I'm worried about, it's my pins. It's my legs. I can't walk!" (*Note: This is an opportunity to bring in a bit of humour. But if using "pins" for "legs" doesn't work in your situation, leave it out.*)

But Jesus knows that the man's sin is a far more pressing problem than his paralysis. To see why, we have to understand what the Bible means by "sin".

Sin isn't just doing wrong things; it's not just lust or laziness or whatever. No, the Bible says that sin is ignoring our Creator in the world he has made. It's living the way *we* want, instead of the way *he* wants. And sin matters because it gets in the way between us and God.

Jesus knows that our relationship with God is more important than anything else. That's why his focus is on the man's sin, rather than his legs.

But as we saw earlier, the religious leaders are furious. They know that only God has the power and authority to forgive sin. If sin is ignoring God in the world he has made, then only God has the right to forgive it. So they take it for granted that Jesus must be lying.

But Jesus knows what they are thinking. So he says to them:

👁 **Read Mark 2:10-12**

The whole point of Jesus healing the man – of doing that amazing creative miracle – is to reveal his true *identity*. To show that he **is** God and that he does have authority on earth to forgive sin.

Next time we will see that Jesus himself said that this is why he came. His mission is to save sinners.

Conclusion

We heard earlier what happens when you get someone's identity wrong.

💬 *Briefly (in one sentence) recap the illustration you used at the beginning of the talk.*

Mark has given us five examples of evidence that point to the real identity of Jesus. We've seen his power and authority to teach; to heal the sick; to control nature; to raise the dead; and to forgive sin. We've seen that Jesus acts in God's world, with God's authority.

So who is Jesus? Mark is showing us that Jesus is God's Son, with the same power and authority as God. And that he is God's only chosen King. And if this is who he is – the question for us is: "How have we been relating to him?"

3: SIN

Why did Jesus come?

Deliver Talk 3 using the notes below. The notes for this talk can also be downloaded from **www.ceministries.org** to enable you to adapt them for your group and add your own illustrations. Alternatively you could show Episode 3 (Sin) from the Christianity Explored DVD if this would be appropriate for your group.

There is a bulleted talk outline on page 19 of the group member's Handbook. Encourage people to write notes next to this outline as they listen to the talk.

Aim

To show that Jesus came to cure our heart problem – our sin – and to rescue us from judgment and hell.

To challenge group members to consider the implications of this for their own lives.

Introduction

Start with an illustration about finding out the truth about ourselves while there's still time to do something about it. If you don't have a personal illustration about this, use the following:

I don't know how you feel about dentists. I suspect that very few of us get up in the morning thinking: "At last, the day I've been looking forward to. I'm off to see the dentist for my six-month check-up!"

You know the dentist's sharp little pick is going to sink in every now and again. And when it does, you feel the pain and you know you're in trouble.

But it's better to know about something rotten now than when it's too late to do anything about it.

Adapt the following paragraph to fit the illustration you have just used.

This session of *Christianity Explored* is going to be a little bit like going to the dentist. Listening to what Jesus has to say about us can be extremely uncomfortable, because, like the dentist's pick, it exposes what we're really like. But it's better to find out the truth about ourselves while we still have time to do something about it.

There are aspects of Jesus' teaching that are difficult for all of us to hear. But these are things we need to know, and Jesus wants us to know about them, because he can deal with them.

We've already explored *who Jesus is*. In this session we focus on another vital question: *Why did Jesus come?*

How would you answer that one? Did he want to bring peace on earth? Was it to heal disease, and end the sufferings of the world? Did he want to transform society, and give us an example of how we ought to live?

There's an element of truth in every one of those options. But Mark says they're not the main reason Jesus came. Jesus came to cure a problem we all have…

1. We all have a heart problem

Start with one or two examples of natural beauty in your location or country, eg: a well-known beauty spot, a rugged mountain range, a waterfall, a beach…

When we look at the world, there's so much to marvel at. But who can honestly say the world is all good?

Estimates vary, but histories of the twentieth century suggest that at least one hundred million people died violently in those hundred years. That's two thousand four hundred violent deaths every day. The question is: Why is the world like this?

Jesus tells us the uncomfortable truth in Mark's Gospel. He says the reason the *world* is not the way it's supposed to be is because *we* are not the way we're supposed to be.

Imagine for a moment a huge public gallery. (You could give an example of a gallery or public building nearby.) On the walls is a display about you. It shows everything you've ever done – and also every word you've said, and every thought you've had. Nothing is left out – it's all there, for everyone to see.

Now I'm sure there will be parts you're proud of: special achievements; success at work or sport or music; times when you've helped others, or been generous with your money.

But there will also be thousands of things that you don't want anyone to see. Things you've done, or said, or thought that you wouldn't want anyone to know about, not even your closest friend.

And it's not only the things we've said, done and thought that are a problem. There are also the things we should have done, and the words we should have said.

I wonder how you would feel, knowing that all of that was exposed for everyone to see. For myself, if my life were on the walls for everyone to see, I'd be so ashamed. I wouldn't be able to look people in the eye. Could you, if you're being honest?

So why are we like this? Why is there so much to be ashamed of? Jesus gives us the answer in Mark chapter 7.

👁 **Read Mark 7:20-23**

What Jesus said is startling. It's like being shown an X-ray of our hearts. Not an X-ray that shows bones, but one that shows who we are and what we are really like inside.

You may feel indignant about the things Jesus says here. It's not how people usually talk about wrongdoing. We are used to hearing people in public life calling the wrong things they have done a "mistake". It gives the impression that their adultery or stealing or lying or whatever wasn't intentional, it was just something that came upon them.

But Jesus says that is nonsense. Sin is not something that I come across "out there" and unintentionally get caught up in. It is something I discover in here (*point to your heart*). I can see it on the X-ray – can you? **We have to look within and take responsibility for what we see.** Jesus tells us that sin – rebelling against God and choosing to go our own way rather than his way – comes "from within", from our "hearts".

And see how Jesus includes all of us. He doesn't just mention immorality, theft, murder and adultery – but also greed, envy, slander, arrogance and folly.

Some sins make front-page headlines in this world. Some don't. But they are all evil in God's reckoning, and they all come from inside you and me! If we could see the gallery of our lives on the walls, we'd see that we all have a heart problem.

Each of us has a heart problem. We often treat each other and our world in a shameful way. But our problems don't end there, because we treat God in that way too.

In Mark chapter 12, Jesus tells us how we *should* relate to God:

👁 **Read Mark 12:30**

If you don't have a heart problem – if you're not a sinner – then you will look back on your life and see that you have loved God with **all** your heart, **all** your soul, **all** your mind, and **all** your strength.

If you're not a sinful person, then there won't have been a single moment when your life didn't joyfully centre on God and his glory.

But I see the gallery of my life, and I can't even find ten consecutive minutes where I have treated God with the love and honour that is rightfully his.

We all have the same heart problem. We should love God with all our heart, soul, mind and strength - because he is our loving Creator. But we never manage to do this.

Instead we've all rebelled against God. He is our loving Creator, but we choose to live our lives our own way rather than his way. We give our hearts to lots of things, but not to our Creator. The Bible calls this "sin".

2. Jesus came to cure our heart problem

So why did Jesus come? Mark's Gospel tells us that Jesus came to cure our heart problem: the problem of our sin.

In chapter 2, Mark tells us what happened when Jesus had dinner at Levi's house. Levi was a tax collector who worked for the Romans. He would have been seen as a traitor by Jewish people, and as a "sinner" by the religious leaders. So why is Jesus having a meal with him?

👁 **Read Mark 2:15-17**

There are two groups of people here in this passage – the "good guys" and the "bad guys".

The "good guys" are the senior religious figures of the day – the teachers of the law and the Pharisees. They looked faultless in religious terms. The "bad guys" are made up of people like Levi, the tax collector, and his friends.

And the question is: Who would you expect Jesus to want to spend time with?

The religious types can't believe that Jesus has chosen to have a meal with tax collectors and their friends. Surely he should be with the religious, not the rebels.

But listen again to what Jesus says in verse 17. This is not a coincidence or a mistake. This is intentional. He says:

"It is not the healthy who need a doctor, but the sick. I have not come to call the righteous, but sinners" (Mark 2:17).

Jesus is at Levi's house on business. And his business is to be the doctor for the spiritually sick. He hasn't come for those who think they are spiritually fit, but for those who know that they are spiritual wrecks.

He says, if you think you're good, if you think you're spiritually healthy, then you won't think you need him. Just as healthy people don't need doctors, so people who think they're good don't need Jesus. The qualification for coming to Jesus is not being good enough but realizing that you're bad enough?

Jesus came for people who know they have a heart problem, and know they need him to cure it.

3. Why does our heart problem matter so much?

Return to the illustration that you used at the start of the talk, and explain what would happen if you didn't take the warning seriously. For example:

If the dentist diagnoses my problem, and explains in lurid detail the treatment for it, I might thank him politely and make a run for it. I might choose to ignore the problem, unless I understand the consequences. So it's important that I understand what will happen if I don't take his warning seriously.

The same is true for us now. We need to understand why our heart problem matters so much, and what the consequences are if we don't do anything about it. And that brings us to one of the most disturbing passages in Mark's Gospel, where we discover what Jesus said about the seriousness of sin.

👁 Read Mark 9:43-47

Can you imagine a situation where it would be better to lose a hand than to keep it? Better to lose one eye than to have two? We've probably all seen pictures of people who've lost arms or legs in accidents or wars. These are shocking images.

So why is Jesus using such extreme language here? Why is he being so shocking? Because he knows that if we reject God throughout our lives, then ultimately God will be right to reject us. If our sin isn't dealt with, it will take us to hell. Jesus lovingly warns us about hell because he does not want us to go there.

In the 21st century many people either dismiss hell as a myth, or treat it as a joke. They joke that they'd much rather be in hell than heaven, because all their friends will be in hell too, and it will be much more fun.

But there's no fun in hell. No friendship either. Hell means being totally separated from God's mercy and blessing. And completely cut off from all the goodness God brings. God is the source of love, joy, friendship, kindness. So in hell there's none of these things. Nothing good is there.

Hell is the place where we face God's judgment for our rebellion against him. You can see why Jesus warns us about hell, and uses such strong language to do so. He knows what hell is really like, and he doesn't want us to go there.

Anyone who conducts funerals knows that people want to hear lots about heaven, but we have no integrity unless we also talk about hell. Hell is the consequence of sin. We've already seen that we all have a heart problem. We all sin. And that means we're all in danger, whether we realize it or not. And that's why Jesus came: to cure our heart problem and rescue us from the consequences of our sin.

➡ *Return again to the illustration you used at the beginning. For example:*

> *I might like my dentist if he tells me my teeth are fine, and I can go on eating lots of chocolate. But if he knows that is not the truth, he is not being friendly. My dentist isn't being cruel when he tells me I have a rotten cavity, and that it needs to be fixed. He doesn't say it to ruin my day, or because he enjoys inflicting pain. He's actually being kind. He's warning me about a problem while there's still time to do something about it. I can choose to listen to him, or take no notice. But if I do ignore him, I know that there will be consequences.*

Jesus doesn't warn us about hell because he's being cruel. He doesn't say it to ruin our day. He lovingly warns us about hell because he does not want us to go there. He knows the consequences of our heart problem. And he loves us so much that he came to save us from those consequences – to rescue us from our sin.

If you understand this, then you're beginning to see why Mark says that Jesus is such good news! He didn't come *"to call the righteous, but sinners."*

The question is: Are we going to listen to Jesus while there's still time to do something about the problem?

4: THE CROSS
Why did Jesus die?

4

Deliver Talk 4 using the notes below. The notes for this talk can also be downloaded from **www.ceministries.org** to enable you to adapt them for your group and add your own illustrations. Alternatively you could show Episode 4 (The cross) from the Christianity Explored DVD if this would be appropriate for your group.

There is a bulleted talk outline on page 28 of the group member's Handbook. Encourage people to write notes next to this outline as they listen to the talk.

Aim

To explain the significance of the cross.

To explore the different reactions to Jesus' death as recorded in Mark's Gospel.

To challenge group members to consider the implications of this for their own lives.

Introduction

Let me begin with a question:

If you think for a moment of all the faiths and philosophies in the world, how many of them celebrate the death of their founder? And how many of them see the death of their founder as the most significant moment in history?

I'm sure you know that I'm talking about the Christian faith – but I wanted to ask the question to show how striking this is. The death of Jesus Christ on the cross is at the very centre of Christianity. But think how strange that is.

Hold up a recent biography of someone famous who is no longer alive. (Libraries are a good source if you don't have anything suitable.) Give one or two brief examples of things the biography tells us about that person's life.

If you look at most biographies, the writers want to talk about their subject's life. Their death is often an inevitable footnote.

⚙ *Show how much of your sample biography is about the person's life, and how much (maybe just a couple of pages, or a paragraph) is about their death.*

And yet, in the four biographies of Jesus' life – the Gospels by Matthew, Mark, Luke and John – one third of each book is about Jesus' death.

Not only that, but Christians never stop talking about the cross. This seems particularly strange because crucifixion, the manner in which Jesus died, was considered terribly shameful.

When someone was crucified, they were severely whipped, nailed to a wooden cross, which was then hoisted into place with the victim attached, and left to die. Crucifixion was deliberately made cruel and gruesome so that any slave who was thinking about rebellion would see the crucified victim and conclude that it could never be worth the risk. It was the ultimate deterrent.

So why is the cross the universally-recognized symbol of Christianity? Christians could have chosen a manger to remind them of Jesus' birth, or perhaps a scroll to remind them of his amazing teaching. But no, it's a cross – a reminder of his death. Why is this? The answer is simple. The cross is how Jesus rescues people.

So today we're going to look at:

⬜ what actually happened when Jesus died on the cross

⬜ what that means

⬜ and how people reacted to it.

But first we'll remind ourselves of why people need to be rescued.

Why do we need to be rescued?

In our last session we saw that each of us has a serious "heart problem". We looked at Mark chapter 7 where Jesus says this:

> *"What comes out of a man is what makes him 'unclean'* [by "unclean" Jesus means "sinful"]. *For from within, out of men's hearts, come evil thoughts, sexual immorality, theft, murder, adultery..."*
> and so the list goes on (Mark 7:20-21).

This means that we're all in danger, whether we realize it or not, because ultimately our sin will lead us to hell.

We also saw the wonderful news that Jesus had said earlier:

> "I have not come to call the righteous, but sinners" (Mark 2:17).

Remember the qualification for coming to Jesus isn't being good enough but realizing we're bad enough. Jesus wants to rescue sinful people like you and me. Today we'll see that he does that by what he achieved for us when he died on the cross.

👁 Read Mark 8:31

So Jesus taught his followers that he must suffer and be rejected. That he must be killed. It was something he had to do. But why? We get the answer in Mark chapter 10 verse 45, where Jesus tells us this:

👁 Read Mark 10:45

So that's what Jesus says he came to do: "to give his life as a ransom for many". Jesus went to his death willingly and deliberately. He knew it was necessary.

To understand exactly what happened – and how Jesus died to ransom, or free, others – we need to read Mark's account of Jesus' death.

👁 Read Mark 15:22–39

We learn three striking things from that passage:

1. God was angry

2. Jesus was abandoned

3. We can be accepted

1. God was angry

Verse 33 says:

> "At the sixth hour darkness came over the whole land until the ninth hour" (Mark 15:33).

Mark is counting hours according to the ancient Jewish system, so the sixth hour would have been noon, the middle of the day. At the moment when the midday sun should have been at its brightest in the sky, darkness fell over the whole land, and remained until three o'clock in the afternoon.

It could not have been an eclipse, because this happened at the Jewish Passover feast – and Passover always fell on a full moon. A solar eclipse can't happen at the same time as a full moon. Also, solar eclipses never last more than about six minutes. This darkness lasted three hours. So, something supernatural was going on.

Time and again in the Bible, light symbolizes God's presence and blessing – while darkness is a sign of God's anger and judgment. So when darkness comes over the land while Jesus is dying, it is a sign that God is angry.

Now, we won't understand this if we see anger as something that is unpredictable and wild – the result of a quick temper. God's anger is not like that. God's anger is his settled, controlled, personal hostility to all that is wrong.

God is a God of holiness, of blazing purity – and he hates what is evil. When it comes to evil, he doesn't lean back in a rocking chair, and pretend nothing has happened. No, wrongdoing matters to God.

How I treat you matters to God. How you treat me matters to God. And how we treat the world matters to God. And for some of you who've been badly treated by other people, I want you to know that it matters to God.

Surely if we care about the injustices we see in the world, we can't expect our loving Creator to care less than we do. And a God who cares about injustice is right to be angry about sin, and right to punish it.

So, as Jesus was dying on the cross, darkness came over the whole land. It was a supernatural sign of God's anger. But that leaves us with a question: What does this have to do with Jesus?

2. Jesus was abandoned

In verse 34, Mark tells us something that Jesus said shortly before he died:

> "And at the ninth hour Jesus cried out in a loud voice, 'Eloi, Eloi, lama sabachthani?' – which means, 'My God, my God, why have you forsaken me?'" (Mark 15:34)

Now there is no doubt that Jesus suffered physical agony on the cross. But what is being spoken about here is spiritual agony – being forsaken or abandoned by God.

As we read Mark's account of the crucifixion and hear this cry from Jesus, we begin to see that on the cross Jesus was in some way "forsaken" or abandoned by God, as God punished sin. God was focusing his anger over our sin on Jesus. Jesus was taking the punishment we deserve.

But Jesus had led a sinless life. In our very first session we read about John the Baptist baptizing Jesus. Mark tells us that God the Father's voice was heard at that time saying:

> "You are my Son, whom I love; with you I am well pleased."
> (Mark 1:11)

And in a later part of Mark's Gospel, God's voice is again heard. This time God says:

> "This is my Son, whom I love. Listen to him!" (Mark 9:7)

Jesus never sinned – he always perfectly obeyed the will of God. The significance of that is enormous as we think about his death on the cross. We have seen that God is angry at our sin. We've now seen that God is punishing Jesus. But clearly Jesus was not being punished for his own sin.

So why was God punishing him? And why did Jesus allow himself to be subjected to this? The answer is that Jesus went through all of this on our behalf, so that we can be rescued. He came to give his life as a ransom for many.

➡ *Use the following illustration (pages 180-181) to explain what happened as Jesus died on the cross.*

What to do	**What to say**

Hold up a blank DVD case in your right hand.

Think back to the public gallery where your whole life is displayed on the walls. They show everything you have ever done, said and thought. Now imagine that everything from that display has been recorded onto this DVD.

There's lots of stuff on here that looks great to us. Perhaps there's a loving home, selfless acts, achievements and success. But there is also a lot on this DVD that you're ashamed of. Things you'd rather people didn't see. We all have secrets that we would hate to have exposed.

The Bible says:

> *"Nothing in all creation is hidden from God's sight. Everything is uncovered and laid bare before the eyes of him to whom we must give account"* (Hebrews 4:13).

And it's not just the way we've treated others, but also the way we've treated God that is recorded.

Hold your left hand out, with your palm facing the ceiling.

Now let's suppose that my left hand represents me, and the ceiling represents God. Between God and me is the record of my sin, and it separates me from God.

Take the DVD and put it flat on your hand.

My sin cuts me off from God. But let me illustrate what happened at the cross.

What to do	**What to say**

Hold out your right hand, facing up. Your left hand should still have the DVD.

Suppose that my right hand represents Jesus – and remember that the ceiling represents God. Jesus lived a sinless life. He always perfectly obeyed the will of God – so there was no barrier between him and God.

But Jesus said that he came to "give his life as a ransom for many". So when he was on the cross, he took my sin.

Now transfer the DVD from the left hand to the right hand.

That's why Jesus cried out: *"My God, my God, why have you forsaken me?"* as he hung on the cross. It wasn't his sin that had separated him from God, because Jesus had never sinned. No, it was *our* sin that made him feel forsaken by God.

In those agonizing moments, Jesus was taking upon himself all the punishment that our sin, everything on this DVD, deserves. He gave himself up as a substitute, to be punished on our behalf.

The Bible says:

> *"We all, like sheep, have gone astray, each of us has turned to his own way; and the LORD has laid on him the iniquity of us all"* (Isaiah 53:6).

Jesus died as my substitute, in my place, taking the punishment I deserve.

Refer to your left hand, now empty, still facing upwards.

How much sin is left? *(Wait for an answer – don't worry if it's a long pause. That will make the point even more clearly.)* Yes that's right, zero. In fact, this is shocking; I can be as sinless in God's sight as Jesus himself!

3. We can be accepted

Let's look again at verses 37 and 38.

👁 **Read Mark 15:37–38**

Mark records the exact moment of Jesus' death – but then he turns our attention to something that happens simultaneously at the temple, which is on the other side of the city. He wants us to understand that the two events are connected in some way.

There was a thirty-foot high curtain in the temple, which was as thick as the span of a man's hand. *(Hold up your hand to show how thick the curtain was.)* When Jesus died, this curtain was torn from top to bottom. Why is that significant?

Well, this thick curtain used to hang in the temple, dividing the people from the place where God was said to live. The curtain was like a big "Do not enter" sign. It said loudly and clearly that it is impossible for sinful people like you and me to walk into God's presence.

Then, suddenly, as Jesus died on the cross, God ripped this curtain in two, from top to bottom. It's as if God is saying: "The way is now open for people to approach me." And that's only possible because Jesus had just paid the price for our sin. Jesus had died as the *"ransom for many"*.

That's what was happening on the cross. Jesus was dying as our substitute, being punished for our sin, so that we can be rescued. Because of the cross, the way is now open for people to approach God. You can see why the cross, the reminder of Jesus' death, is the symbol of Christianity.

But what about the people who were there when Jesus died? How did they respond to Jesus' death on the cross?

Four reactions to Jesus' death

Mark brings our attention to the way various people react to the death of Jesus. As we look at these reactions, ask yourself what you see when you look at Jesus' death and how you respond.

1. The soldiers

Verse 24 tells us about the soldiers who had nailed Jesus to the cross.

👁 Read Mark 15:24

The soldiers weren't interested in what was happening on the cross – they had seen it all before. The only thing they were interested in was gambling for Jesus' clothes. They completely missed what was happening right in front of their eyes. For them the main legacy of the cross was Jesus' clothing.

2. The religious leaders

The religious leaders had wanted for a long time to have Jesus killed. They watched him die, laughing about it among themselves.

👁 Read Mark 15:31-32

The religious leaders were convinced that they knew the way to God, so they didn't need Jesus. They knew that some people thought that Jesus was the Christ, God's only chosen King – but the chief priests and teachers of the law refused to believe that.

Ironically they mocked Jesus, claiming that he couldn't save himself – and completely missing the point that he was actually dying to save others, just as he had said he would.

3. Pontius Pilate

So the religious leaders rejected Jesus – but what about the political leader? What about the Roman governor, Pontius Pilate? He had questioned Jesus himself, and knew that Jesus was an innocent man. But Pilate was swayed by the crowds.

👁 Read Mark 15:12-15

Pilate knew that Jesus was innocent. But when the pressure was on, he gave in. Instead of releasing Jesus, as he knew was right, he gave in to the crowds and had Jesus crucified.

By showing us these different reactions it's as if Mark is saying: "OK, this is how others reacted to Jesus' death on the cross. But what about you? What do you see when you look at the cross?"

▣ Are we too busy like the soldiers?

▣ Too self-righteous like the religious leaders?

▣ Too cowardly like Pilate?

But there's one more response to look at...

4. The Roman centurion

Mark records the reaction of a Roman centurion – a hard-bitten soldier who was a high-ranking military officer. He would have seen many men die – but he had never seen a man die like this. This is how Mark describes it:

👁 **Read Mark 15:39**

And that is what we are meant to see as we look at what happened at the cross. We can recognize that Jesus is telling the truth: that he is indeed the Son of God. And that his death is God's amazing plan to rescue us from our sin.

There has never been better news than this. The gospel message tells me the terrible truth about myself – about my heart problem that I cannot cure. But then it tells me the wonderful news about Jesus dying for sinners, to give his life as a ransom for many.

So the question is: What do you make of all this? And what will you do with your sin?

Will you take it with you to the grave, and insist that you pay for it yourself?

Or will you take it to the cross to be forgiven?

5: RESURRECTION

Why did Jesus rise?

Deliver Talk 5 using the notes below. The notes for this talk can also be downloaded from **www.ceministries.org** to enable you to adapt them for your group and add your own illustrations. Alternatively you could show Episode 5 (Resurrection) from the Christianity Explored DVD if this would be appropriate for your group.

There is a bulleted talk outline on page 36 of the group member's Handbook. Encourage people to write notes next to this outline as they listen to the talk.

Aim

To present the facts about the resurrection of Jesus.

To show how the resurrection brings both hope and a warning.

To challenge group members to consider the implications of this for their own lives.

Introduction

Opening illustration. Give a personal example of lining up in a queue, preferably for something you're not looking forward to but will definitely happen. For example:

I remember very vividly when the school doctor came to give us our BCG injections against tuberculosis. Having to stand there, waiting to be injected, wasn't a great feeling. I remember looking at the guys ahead of me in the queue, lined up in alphabetical order. I thought: "If they get in and out alright, then I'll be fine".

The first boy went in, and to my amazement there were no screams from the medical room – and no blood seeping under the door. He came out calmly doing up his shirt cuff, and I thought: "I'm fine. If he can get through it, I can too."

We're running Christianity Explored because we're all in a queue. We are mortal and we will all die – but not necessarily in alphabetical order! We all know this. We can't ignore it, or pretend it's not true, though many try to do so. The fact of death applies to us all – one day our lives will be over.

Last time we saw that Jesus died on a cross to cure our heart problem, the problem of our sin. But Mark tells us that Jesus not only died for sinners, but rose again from death. And because of that, the ultimate terror of death is removed. Because Jesus got through death, and triumphed over it, he can get us through it too.

We're going to trace the events of the resurrection morning from Mark's brief record of it in chapter 16. But first, we'll see what Jesus said about his resurrection **before** it happened.

Jesus knew he would rise again

In these predictions Jesus is again using the phrase "the Son of Man" to talk about himself.

👁 **Read Mark 8:31**

Jesus said the same thing on two other occasions:

> He said to them, "The Son of Man is going to be betrayed into the hands of men. They will kill him, and **after three days he will rise**" (Mark 9:31).

> "We are going up to Jerusalem," he said, "and the Son of Man will be betrayed to the chief priests and teachers of the law. They will condemn him to death and hand him over to the Gentiles, who will mock him and spit on him, flog him and kill him. **Three days later he will rise**" (Mark 10:33-34).

Jesus repeatedly claimed that he would be raised to life on the third day after his death. The resurrection wasn't a surprise to him – he knew his death wouldn't be the end.

So let's see what Mark tells us about the resurrection of Jesus, starting with some women who had watched him die.

👁 **Read Mark 15:40 – 16:3**

📋 *If possible, show the following four headings as a visual aid as you give the talk, revealing each heading as you reach it:*

1. **Dead and buried**
2. **Alive and well**
3. **Ruling as King**
4. **Go and tell**

1. Dead and buried

These women knew Jesus well. We learn in verse 41 that they had cared for Jesus and looked after his needs. And now they watched his gruesome death, and saw where his body was buried.

Jesus was buried by a man called Joseph of Arimathea. He went to the Roman governor, Pontius Pilate, and rather bravely asked permission to bury the body.

Pilate was surprised to hear that Jesus had died already. So he checked the facts. He asked the Roman centurion if Jesus was in fact dead – and the centurion confirmed that it was true. So Pilate agreed that Joseph could take the body.

Joseph took the lifeless, bloodied body down from the cross, wrapped it in linen, and placed it in a tomb cut out of rock. Jesus Christ was dead and buried.

But now it was 36 hours later on the Sunday morning, and these three grieving women came to do what they imagined was the last loving thing they could do for him. They came to embalm his corpse.

Some time after dark the previous evening, when the Jewish Sabbath was over and the shops were opening again, they had gone and bought some spices. Their idea was to put them on the linen that the body was wrapped in, as a last loving act, to mask the smell of decay.

So they got up first thing the next morning, and set off to the tomb. They already knew where to go because they had seen the burial of Jesus.

As they made their way to the grave, they discussed the barrier they were going to face that morning. They had seen Joseph roll the very large stone across the entrance to the tomb, and wondered who might roll the stone away again so that they could put their spices on the body. It would have been too heavy for them to move themselves – even harder than one of us trying to lift a piano on our own.

You might include a personal illustration here of visiting a grave of someone you knew and loved. You know you won't see that person there; you know that they are dead; but you go to remember them, and maybe put some flowers on the grave.

That's how it was for the women that morning, because they knew – just like the Roman centurion – that Jesus was dead and buried.

2. Alive and well

Let's have a look at the next part of chapter 16 to see what happened when the women reached the tomb.

👁 **Read Mark 16:4-8**

The women were given two staggering shocks which left them *"trembling and bewildered"* (v 8), and they *"fled from the tomb"*. The Greek word translated as "fled" is the word used for escaping from a wild animal. If you can imagine how you'd feel being chased by a bull or a pack of wolves, then you know how these women felt!

➡ *If you have a personal illustration of being chased by an animal, use it briefly here. eg: "I was chased by an angry dog once, and was terrified. That's how these women felt."*

The first shock comes in verse 4 when the women arrive and find that the stone in front of the tomb has been dealt with. The huge heavy stone has been flung away from the entrance.

The second shock is that there's no need for the spices they've spent so much money on. The barrier has been removed – and the body isn't there.

Then the *"young man dressed in a white robe"* – who is clearly a messenger from God – says this:

> *"Don't be alarmed … You are looking for Jesus the Nazarene, who was crucified"* (Mark 16:6).

So he confirmed that a man from Nazareth, called Jesus, whose death the women had seen, had been crucified and was buried there. He says:

> *"See the place where they laid him."*

They were not imagining this, they were not in the wrong place – that's the place where Jesus was laid. They were not dreaming – it really happened. But it's not the end of the story.

The messenger says: "You can see the place, you can see the discarded grave clothes, but you won't see him. He's not here. He is risen!"

But that's not the end of the young man's news. He has a message for the disciples – one that can only be true if Jesus really has risen from the dead.

> *"But go, tell his disciples and Peter, 'He is going ahead of you into Galilee. There you will see him, just as he told you'"* (Mark 16:7).

One of the predictions we looked at in our "Explore" study earlier was Jesus telling his disciples that he would rise to life, and then go to Galilee, where they would join him. Now the young man in white is telling the women the same thing. The risen Jesus would meet the disciples, including Peter, in Galilee.

Mark ends his book with the reaction of the women. But the other three Gospels, and the book of Acts, fill in some of the things that happened after the resurrection. They tell us that Jesus appeared to his disciples on at least ten separate occasions after his death. He also appeared to more than 500 people at the same time.

Now, at this point you may find it hard to believe what Mark tells us about the resurrection. Or perhaps you dismiss everything the Bible says about the amazing things Jesus said and did. We all know that bringing life to a corpse is something that human science and power can't do. But we should not reject the resurrection of the dead on the grounds that we can't do it.

Please don't discard the plain teaching of the Bible about Jesus dying and rising on the basis that if we can't do it, it can't be done. As we meet Jesus in Mark's Gospel we hear and see things that are well beyond our comprehension and ability. **But that's what you would expect when God the Son comes into the world he has created.**

But if you haven't seen who Jesus is as he teaches and calls and heals and controls and raises from death and forgives sins – then of course you will not believe he can be raised from death.

Mark doesn't "rose-tint" the reactions of the original hearers of the news that Jesus had risen. The women had seen Jesus brutally executed 36 hours earlier. They react to the news that he is alive again with bewilderment and fear. Mark doesn't down-play their struggle to comprehend what they are being told about Jesus. Because this is history – this happened!

3. Ruling as King

Think about all of the things that were done to Jesus before and as he died. People betrayed him, rejected him, mocked him, spat on him, flogged him, and killed him. These things show what those people thought of Jesus. He was worthless to them. They attached no value to his life.

But the resurrection shows that God has reversed that verdict. He places ultimate worth on his Son. God did not leave Jesus where men had laid him. No, the startling news came: *"He is risen!"* God thinks differently about his Son. People rejected him – God has lifted him up. This was always the plan.

It was because of this that the man from heaven said in verse 7:

> "But go, tell his disciples and Peter, 'He is going ahead of you into Galilee. There you will see him, just as he told you.'"

Jesus always spoke about the certainty of his resurrection when he spoke about his death. What a picture this is of the sovereign power of Jesus the King. Who else could be in such control of every aspect of his death and resurrection?

It's almost as though Jesus had been saying to his followers: "We're going to have a really tough time, and you will see me die – but I am rising on Sunday, and we will all meet up in Galilee on Monday as planned."

Anyone could say these words, but only a King of staggering power could make them happen!

So the resurrection of Jesus reverses the world's verdict on Jesus. It shows that he is God's exalted Son and King – who was always in sovereign control, even as he was being rejected by the Jews, abandoned by the disciples, brutalised by the Romans, and forsaken by God on the cross as He paid for my sin.

The women had come to pay their last loving tribute to a dead body; to anoint a corpse. They thought that everything had finished in this tragedy as Christ was murdered and their hopes were shattered.

But now those three words "He has risen" change everything.

4. Go and tell

We have seen how uncompromisingly honest Mark is in his record of what happened that day. Mark 16:8 tells us that, at least initially, the women were so completely overwhelmed that they ran for their lives and said nothing.

Nevertheless, you can see that this news of the resurrection needs to be told. God's messenger had said:

> "But go, tell his disciples and Peter, 'He is going ahead of you into Galilee. There you will see him, just as he told you.'" (Mark 16:7)

In other words, the news is: Jesus is alive, and you are going to meet him, just as he said.

◼ *If possible, show this statement as a visual aid:*

The news is: Jesus is alive, and you are going to meet him, just as he said.

How could anyone say that the Christian message is irrelevant to them? We are all in that queue – we will all have to face death. Yet here is Jesus – who walked out of the grave to lead those who trust him out of the grave too.

The news of the resurrection is utterly wonderful. It means death didn't destroy Jesus; he suffered it, and then destroyed it by rising. This news is amazing and wonderful.

But this is the point where it gets uncomfortable for all of us. I am uncomfortable, because I have to tell you something, and I am concerned that you do not mishear me. And you will be uncomfortable as you listen, because the resurrection of Jesus has another implication.

So let me say it again, and then explain it. This news of the resurrection must be told. The news is: Jesus is alive, and **you are** going to meet Him, just as He said.

Do you see the inescapable implication of the resurrection for everyone? It is not just the disciples who will see Jesus again – we all will.

In Acts 17, when the apostle Paul was speaking in Athens, he said that God *"has set a day when he will judge the world with justice by the man he has appointed. He has given proof of this to all men **by raising him from the dead**"* (Acts 17:31).

The resurrection of Jesus brings hope in the face of death. But it also promises that Jesus Christ has the power and the right to raise us and judge us. There will be an end point in history, where Jesus returns to this world – which is still in rebellion against him – and ends that rebellion. There must come a day when God shows that the despised Jesus is his beloved, exalted Son, King and Judge.

Now that is a terrifying prospect if you, like me, know how badly you have treated the Lord Jesus.

🔲 *Hold up the DVD from last week's illustration, and remind the group that this holds a record of everything we have done, said and thought.*

But let me close by showing you from Mark 16 how you can be ready and una-shamed to meet Jesus when he returns.

Mark 16:7 says: *"But go, tell his disciples **and Peter**, 'He is going ahead of you into Galilee. There you will see him, just as he told you.'"*

🔲 *Hold up the DVD again.*

What was on Peter's DVD? The disciples had all fled from Jesus at the critical time. But Peter had denied even knowing him. This is the man who argued in Mark 8 that Jesus should not go to the cross. But notice how, after Peter's failure, the risen Jesus sends a particular message to Peter.

Peter would have thought his failure was final. But the risen Lord Jesus has died for sins, and says that Peter is welcome.

Even though, like Peter, we have denied God and made a mess of our relationship with him, Jesus paid for that sin on the cross. And now he lives – as the resurrection proves – to forgive all those who will trust him.

The resurrection proves that God has accepted the death of Jesus in my place, in full and final payment for my personal rebellion against him. Jesus gave his life as a ransom for many, just as he said he would. He died to pay for our sin, and rose again to prove that sin was truly paid for. The ransom price has been paid.

So this is the message that everyone needs to hear: Jesus is alive, and you are going to meet him, just as he said.

But you can meet him before then, by faith. And as you thank him for dying for you, ask his forgiveness for your sin, and put your life in his hands, you can go through life with no fear of death or judgment because Jesus faced it for you.

Because of the resurrection, we can trust Jesus with our own death. And because he is alive, you can speak to him yourself right now.

🔲 *Either give a quick personal testimony about "meeting Jesus by faith" and "speaking to him yourself" – and how real and transforming that is.*
Or suggest that people can ask you or one of the other leaders about this at the end of the session if they want to find out more.

Let me end by saying again that this is the message that everyone needs to hear: Jesus is alive, and **you are** going to meet him, just as he said.

6: GRACE

How can God accept us?

- *Deliver Talk 6 using the notes below. The notes for this talk can also be downloaded from www.ceministries.org to enable you to adapt them for your group and add your own illustrations. Alternatively you could show Episode 6 (Grace) from the Christianity Explored DVD if this would be appropriate for your group.*

- *There is a bulleted talk outline on page 43 of the group member's Handbook. Encourage people to write notes next to this outline as they listen to the talk.*

- *This talk uses 14 large cards (or sheets of paper) as visual aids. Leave one card blank. Write the following on the remaining cards (or download a set from www.ceministries.org):*

Set A:	Set B:
I'm a good person	I'm a spiritual person
I don't steal	I try to treat others as I like to be treated myself
I don't lie	I've been baptised
I give to charity	I go to church
I give blood	I go to communion
I'm not a murderer	I read the Bible
I'm not a rapist	

Aim

- To show that we can never do enough to inherit eternal life

- To explain God grace – his undeserved gift to us

- To look at the implications of this for how group members respond to God

Introduction

At the beginning of *Christianity Explored* we asked you this:

"If you could ask God one question, and you knew it would be answered, what would it be?"

Now I'd like you to think about another question. This time it's something that God might ask you:

"If God were to say to you: 'Why should I give you eternal life?', what would you say?"

Take a few moments to think quietly about your answer.

⊞ *(Optional) You might like to ask group members to write their answers down, assuring them that they won't be asked to read them out. If you do this, give the group an opportunity to think about the question again at the beginning of the "Discuss" section after this talk, since they may want to change their answers.*

I wonder what your answer was. Some answers people may give are as follows:

⊞ *Hold up the cards from Set A one at a time. This works well if you hold up the whole set, and then move each card in turn from the front to the back.*

Or maybe yours is a more religious answer:

⊞ *Hold up the cards from Set B one at a time. Then put the cards down in a pile to use again later.*

The question of eternal life is one that many people think about at some point in their lives. I'd guess that you probably wouldn't still be doing this course if you weren't interested in knowing the answer.

In Mark 10 we discover some crucial things about eternal life. And we also find it described in a number of different ways: "having treasure in heaven", "entering the kingdom of God", "being saved". All of these mean being accepted by God as a member of his kingdom now, and looking forward to enjoying a relationship with him for ever.

In Mark 10 we meet a man who really wanted to know how to have eternal life. Mark tells us that this man had "great wealth". Two other Bible writers help us to build a picture of him: Matthew tells us that he is young, and Luke adds the detail that he is a "ruler" of some kind.

So this man seems to have everything going for him. He's young; despite his youth he's already an important man; and he's very wealthy. But he has a crucial question to ask Jesus – about something he knows he doesn't have – eternal life.

👁 **Read Mark 10:17**

Notice two things this young man says to Jesus: he calls Jesus *"Good teacher"* and he asks what he has to *"do"* to inherit eternal life. Jesus picks up on both of these as he helps this man to understand some very important things.

The problem with "being good"

Firstly, Jesus focuses on the title "Good teacher".

👁 **Read Mark 10:18**

Maybe the man was just being polite. He knew Jesus had built a reputation as someone who taught with authority, and whose teaching was completely different from that of the religious leaders. And he clearly respected Jesus as a man of God – so much so that he fell on his knees before Jesus. So maybe "Good teacher" was his way of showing respect for Jesus.

But Jesus chose to use the title to teach this man – and also the disciples, who were listening in. *"No-one is good – except God alone,"* he said. Notice what Jesus is **not** saying. He's not denying his deity – he's not saying that he isn't God's Son. Jesus is indeed **good**. But he is also using this title to challenge how most people see themselves.

It's easy to compare ourselves to someone who is dishonest, or violent, or a sex offender, and to decide that compared to them we're basically good. We use the word "good" when we mean "not as bad as".

💬 *Give an illustration of someone currently in the news for fraud, sex offences, murder etc. Explain that one reason the media have focused so strongly on this person is because we're shocked at their level of wrongdoing. Compared to them, most of us would say that we live good lives.*

But Jesus shows that we're comparing ourselves to the wrong person. The question isn't whether we're better than _____ (*the person you've just spoken about*). The issue is how we match up to God himself. He is genuinely and completely good. He is perfectly just, perfectly wise, perfectly pure and perfectly loving. As Jesus puts it: *"No-one is good – except God alone."*

Now it seems likely that this man did consider himself to be good. Let's see how Jesus draws that out of him.

👁 **Read Mark 10:19-20**

The laws Jesus gives here come from the ten commandments. These were ten laws that God gave to Moses to show the Israelites how to live as God's people. The commands Jesus quotes are all about how we relate to those around us. There were also commands about how to relate to God, which Jesus will come to later.

The rich young man was very confident about his ability to keep God's commands. He declared: *"All these I have kept since I was a boy"*.

▪ *Hold up the full set of cards (Sets A and B together) again.*

His answer would have been some of the things we've seen on these cards. In other words, he'd treated people well. He had never murdered anyone, or committed adultery. He wasn't a thief, a cheat or a liar. He was a good son to his mum and dad. He was supremely confident that he'd lived a good life, keeping God's laws.

If God were to say to this man: "Why should I give you eternal life?", that's the answer the man would give.

Why good is never enough

The young man's law-keeping gives us a clue to the second thing he asked Jesus:

*"Good teacher … what must I **do** to inherit eternal life?"* (Mark 10:17)

He already kept the laws Jesus had listed – or believed that he did. But surely there was something else he could do to inherit eternal life. In other words, he wanted to know how he could *earn* a place in God's kingdom, how he could be good enough for God to accept him. He wanted to be able to work for it, and to receive it as a well-deserved reward.

▪ *Give an example of something you have worked for and achieved: eg: passing a teaching certificate to work in schools; taking a computer qualification to earn a promotion; passing your driving test, or learning guitar to play in a band. We're used to earning our success – and it seems that this young man wanted to do the same thing.*

This rich young man seemed to genuinely believe that he was fully keeping all of God's laws. And that maybe there was something else he could do to earn eternal life. He wanted to be told what to *do* – so Jesus answered him.

196

👁 Read Mark 10:21-22

This man has asked Jesus what to do. But when Jesus tells him, he doesn't respond with joy or a desire to do it as quickly as possible. Instead, his face falls, he turns away, and goes home sad. Why? Because *"he had great wealth"*.

He was rich, and being asked to give away all his money was too much for him. What this actually shows is that he isn't keeping all of God's laws at all. The first commandments are about how we relate to God. They include this:

> *"You shall have no other gods before me. You shall not make for yourself*
> *an idol in the form of anything in heaven above or on the earth beneath*
> *or in the waters below. You shall not bow down to them or worship*
> *them"* (Exodus 20:3-5).

In other words, no one is greater than God. And you mustn't treat anyone or anything as more important than him. If this rich young ruler really thought that loving and serving God, and enjoying eternal life, was more important than the things he had on earth, he would have gladly given away his money, and given up his importance, to follow Jesus. The point is that if anyone is going to earn eternal life, they would have to live perfectly, in relation to others, and in relation to God.

The man's reaction shows that he isn't keeping all of God's laws at all – he is treating his money as an idol, as more important than the God who made him. There is a greater treasure he'd rather have than being with Jesus and having treasure in heaven. His money is more important to him than God.

So we see that this man was wrong in believing that he was fully keeping God's laws. But he was also wrong in thinking that he could do something to earn eternal life. We can never do enough to inherit eternal life. Look at what Jesus says next:

👁 Read Mark 10:23-27

At this time people believed that wealth and success were proof that God was pleased with you. So the disciples were stunned by what Jesus said. If even rich men found it hard to enter the kingdom of God, how could anyone else possibly do it?

So they ask their own question. And it's the right question to ask. Not "what can I *do* to be saved" but "who then *can* be saved?". And Jesus replies: *"With man this is impossible"*.

The problem with our hearts

Do you remember in session 3 that we learned that we all have a heart problem.

> *"For from within, out of men's hearts, come evil thoughts, sexual immorality, theft, murder, adultery, greed, malice, deceit, lewdness, envy, slander, arrogance and folly. All these evils come from inside and make a man 'unclean'"* (Mark 7:21-23).

Sin comes from within, from our hearts – and we all sin. We don't love God with all our heart, soul, mind and strength. We have a heart problem, and nothing we do can cure it. This is why Jesus came. He came *"to serve, and to give his life as a ransom for many"* (Mark 10:45). Jesus came to rescue us from our sin, by taking the punishment we deserve.

And we know that the ransom price was paid and accepted because of the resurrection. Jesus died to pay for sin, and rose from death to prove that sin was truly paid for.

This is why Jesus says: *"With man this is impossible"*. Nothing we do can cure our heart problem – only Jesus can.

🔲 *Hold up the full set of cards again. Either rip them in half or throw them onto the ground one at a time to show that they are useless.*

But what then is the answer to the disciples' question? *"Who then can be saved?"*

God's amazing gift

The answer to that question comes from another meeting with Jesus. Just before the rich young ruler came to Jesus, some other people were brought to him. They weren't rich, important or even adults: they were little children.

🔲 *Give an illustration of how young children are seen in your country and culture. For example, in the UK there are more and more television adverts aimed at children and young teenagers. Children have more money of their own to spend, and advertisers are also aware of their "pester power" to persuade their parents to buy them the latest gadgets, fashions, games etc. You could quote or show a recent advert of this kind.*

In first-century Israel children were seen very differently. They were greatly loved by their parents, but also seen as a burden on the family resources until they were old enough to work. Children had little or no status. Keep that in mind as we read again the passage we looked at earlier in our group.

👁 Read Mark 10:13-16

These children had nothing to offer Jesus. They hadn't done anything to deserve his love and acceptance. Perhaps that's why the disciples didn't want Jesus to be bothered by them. But listen to what Jesus says:

> "…the kingdom of God belongs to such as these … anyone who will not receive the kingdom of God like a child will never enter it"
> (Mark 10:14-15).

These children did nothing to *earn* acceptance by Jesus.

🖥 *Hold up a blank card.*

All they did was come to him. And Jesus took them in his arms. He put his hands on them, and he blessed them.

How to receive God's gift

Here is the answer to the rich man's question about inheriting eternal life. And to the disciples' question about being saved. The answer is that only those who receive the kingdom of God *like a child* will enter it.

🖥 *Give a personal illustration of giving someone a gift, a child if possible. Include how they responded. For example, giving a present to your own child, or god-child, or a niece or nephew, and describing their excitement when opening it. Explain how shocked you would have been if the child had asked how much they had to pay for the present. They didn't need to pay anything – it was a gift.*

We can't do anything to earn eternal life. We can't work our way into the kingdom of God. Nothing we do can cure our heart problem. We can't do anything ourselves in order to be saved. But we can receive it as a free gift – paid for by the death of Jesus.

Our entry point to God's kingdom is not the good things we've done for God. Rather, it's the amazing thing Christ has done for us. It's not about getting what we think we have earned, but rather it is about us receiving from God the opposite of what we deserve. The Bible calls this "grace" – God's undeserved gift to us. And like a child, all we can do is receive it.

Conclusion

This is the good news that Mark wrote about at the very beginning of his book: the good news about Jesus Christ.

Jesus shows us that we are all sinful. We all have a heart problem that we can't cure. He tells us that there is nothing we can do to be saved. But he also showed how much he loves us by willingly dying to take the punishment we deserve, to give his life as a ransom for many. And as a result, when we trust in what Jesus has done, we can be accepted by God and be given eternal life – if we will just receive it as a free, undeserved gift.

That's grace – that we are more sinful than we ever imagined, but more loved than we ever dreamed.

And the impact of grace on our lives *now* is enormous. Living by grace means I don't need to go through life pretending to be what I'm not or wearing masks to disguise who I am. When I understand God's grace, I have nothing to prove and no masks to wear any more. God knows exactly what I'm like. I can't hide it from him. And yet, amazingly, in Christ he accepts and loves me. That is so liberating. It is such good news!

That's grace.

DAY AWAY 1: THE SOWER
Listen carefully

*Deliver Day Away Talk 1 using the notes below. The notes for this talk can also be downloaded from **www.ceministries.org** to enable you to adapt them for your group and add your own illustrations. Alternatively you could show Episode 7 (The Sower) from the* Christianity Explored *DVD if this would be appropriate for your group.*

There is a bulleted talk outline on page 50 of the group member's Handbook. Encourage people to write notes next to this outline as they listen to the talk.

Aim

- To show that the good news of Jesus will only change your life if you hear it properly.
- To challenge group members to consider what kind of soil they are.

Introduction

The whole *Christianity Explored* course is built around the three big questions Mark is fascinated by: Who is Jesus? Why did he come? What is involved in following him?. In the first two sessions we explored **who Jesus is**. Then in Sessions 3-5 we saw **why Jesus came**. The question from Session 6 on is: How should we respond? **What does Jesus ask of us?**

In order to answer that question we need to get something very basic in place:

Have we heard what Jesus says? Has his word taken root in our lives?

That is the issue in Mark chapter 4. Jesus tells a story that pictures his extraordinary, life-changing words as tiny, vulnerable seeds. What Jesus is saying is clear. Just as seeds will only grow if you plant them properly, so the good news about him will only change your life… if you hear it properly.

👁 **Read Mark 4:3-9**

I don't know if you realized it, but you had a walk-on part in that story. Everyone who has ever heard the good news – the gospel message about Jesus – appears in it. It's as if Jesus is holding up a mirror so that we can see ourselves reflected back.

The main focus of the parable is not on the sower, or the seed. Jesus focuses on the soil. It is all about where the seed lands – the way that people respond to hearing the gospel message, and how Satan interferes with God's word to prevent it from making its impact.

Jesus likens us to four different types of soil the seed falls on – the hard soil on the path, the shallow soil on the rock, the soil in which thorns grow, and lastly good soil. Each of us receives the good news in a different way. And Jesus wants us to ask ourselves the question: How am I responding to the gospel? What kind of soil am I?

Hard ground

The first type of soil is in verse 4: the path, where the soil is hard. The fields in ancient Israel were long, narrow strips divided by little paths. Over the years, the constant traffic of footsteps, hooves and wheels turned these paths as hard as concrete. So if seeds fell here, they'd never go deep into the soil – they'd just bounce off and remain on the surface.

When the seed falls on this hard ground, the birds immediately come and eat it up.

Jesus explains in verse 15 that some people, as they hear the good news about Jesus, are just like that hardened path:

> "As soon as they hear it, Satan comes and takes away the word that was sown in them" (Mark 4:15).

You may never have taken the person of Satan, the devil, seriously before. You may have thought he was a mythical figure from fairy tales. But the Bible says he is utterly real. All the way through Mark's Gospel we see Jesus encountering him and defeating his power. And here Jesus warns *us* to take Satan seriously, and to be aware of the subtlety of his work. Satan's aim is always to stop the gospel message from being properly heard, and to take it from us – immediately if possible.

The person who is like this first type of soil, the path, may be a hardened sceptic who immediately rejects anything that challenges their own ideas.

Or it may simply be someone who is easily distracted. Satan loves to distract us with thoughts about work, family, finance or hobbies. If he can only distract you so that the word of God goes in one ear and out the other, he will have successfully taken away God's message and blocked its impact on you.

■ *Add a personal illustration about someone rejecting or being distracted from the gospel message. For example:*

I took a friend along to a meeting to hear a well-known speaker explain the gospel. At the end of the evening when I asked him for his thoughts on what was said, he explained that he couldn't take anyone seriously who had an accent like that speaker! He had switched off immediately.

There is a large, yellow sign chained to a lamppost just off Oxford Circus in central London. In black writing it bears this message...

> *"Thieves operate in this area. You are not obliged to be their victim. Guard your valuables!"*

As we begin our day together, I want to issue the same warning. There is a thief among us who wants to take from you – not your wallet, purse or car keys – but the word of God. There is a risk of us going home at the end of the day with an empty head and heart, because everything of lasting significance has been stolen from us. Satan is like a thief who wants to take the gospel message from you.

Do you recognize the possibility that so far the truth of the gospel message, the power of God's word, has fallen on hard ground in your life? If you can't really remember much from the course, and if little of what we have seen about Jesus has made an impact on you, then you have been robbed of the truth. Please talk to me, or your group leader, if you are concerned about this.

But the thief is not limited to an immediate snatch. Sometimes he works more gradually – slowly, secretly, taking the seed of God's word from our lives.

Shallow ground

In Israel, some of the land has a thin layer of soil lying on the top of limestone bedrock. If seed falls there, the sun heats the soil quickly because it's so shallow, and the seed responds at once. The immediate growth is spectacular.

But the bedrock only a few inches below means there's nothing for the roots to go down into, and no way for the plant to get moisture. So it quickly dies.

That is what Jesus had in mind in verse 5. And he explains it in verses 16-17:

👁 **Read Mark 4:16-17**

This person responds quickly and joyfully to the gospel message. But then trouble or persecution come as a result – at which point they fall away, they give up on following Jesus.

It is amazing to see how candid Jesus is. He fully expects and warns us that trouble and persecution will come. Jesus himself was rejected, and his followers will be too. That can be very painful.

This trouble is a bit like the side-effects you get with some medications. Many life-saving treatments bring with them some pretty awful side-effects.

📝 *Give a personal illustration of someone (yourself?) experiencing distressing side-effects from life-saving treatment such as chemotherapy.*

There are times when the patient undergoing treatment may wonder if the cure is worse than the condition. But to give up on the life-saving treatment because of the temporary side-effects would be to give up on life.

Like a doctor, Jesus explains the unpleasant temporary side-effects of following him. He warns us that if we have not understood and expected this hostile reaction from people, we may decide that the trouble attracted by the Christian life is not worth it. We may give up on Jesus rather than put up with the cost of following him.

That is why we are careful during *Christianity Explored* to explain what it means to follow Jesus; that there will be tough times for us. The Christian life is like climbing up the down escalator. We have to go against the flow. There will be many obstacles and much opposition.

📝 *Ask a leader to give a three-minute testimony at this point about the tough time they faced after becoming a Christian.*

But we won't be left to cope with this on our own. Back in Mark chapter 1 we read that Jesus *"will baptise you with the Holy Spirit"* (Mark 1:8). The Holy Spirit isn't a force, like electricity. He is a person. He is God's Spirit, who comes to live in everyone who follows Jesus. He gives those who trust in Jesus the power to get through the tough times and the roots to stabilize us.

Thorny ground

I have never known a gardener choose to grow thorns and weeds. But according to Jesus that's what people in this third category effectively do in their lives.

👁 **Read Mark 4:18-19**

"The worries of this life" are not so much negative things we are worried about, but the things which distract and preoccupy us so much that they grow to define us.

Desire for security, comfort, approval or power, maybe money, maybe the desire for a potential spouse who doesn't share their view of Jesus – these desires, and the worries that come with them, become stronger than the desire for Jesus.

Jesus also mentions the *"deceitfulness of wealth"*. Wealth is deceitful when it promises complete happiness and guarantees a meaningful life. We become deceived when we make becoming wealthy – or at least wealthier than we are at the moment – the priority of our lives.

We may get that niggling feeling that if we stick with the gospel, and build our lives on it, we will have to give up something much better.

It's like the story of the young man who said: "Darling, I want you to know that I love you more than anything else in the world. Will you marry me? I know I'm not rich like John Brown, I don't have a big house or a beautiful car, but I do love you with all my heart." And the young woman replies: "I love you with all my heart too – but tell me more about John Brown."

The *"desire for other things"* may cause us to believe that we would be much happier if we don't get too serious about Jesus.

The desire for other things competes with our involvement with Jesus. When we are like thorny ground, we don't see that the security, comfort, approval and power that come from knowing Christ infinitely outweigh any treasure the world has to offer.

Good ground

The seed of God's word must be great and powerful if Satan has set up all these strategies against it. In the final verse of the parable Jesus shows us the astonishing effectiveness and power of the gospel message to radically change lives. In verse 20 Jesus says:

> *"Others, like seed sown on good soil, hear the word, accept it, and produce a crop – thirty, sixty or even a hundred times what was sown"* (Mark 4:20).

When Jesus talks about the fourth kind of soil in this parable, he's talking about someone who not only hears the good news about Jesus Christ, but sees it for what it is and makes it their treasure. When Jesus himself becomes more valuable to you than anything else in the world, that's when you know you've really heard him. And from tiny beginnings, as the seed of God's word begins to grow in our lives, changes are made that last for eternity.

In a cemetery in Italy there is a thick marble slab over the top of one of the graves. But, somehow, years earlier, an acorn had fallen through a small crack into the grave. And over the years the acorn had grown until eventually it had smashed through the surface of the hard marble and cracked the enormous slab into two pieces. As the tree grew up, it just pushed the marble aside as if it wasn't there.

There's a lot of power packed into that seed. All it needed was the right kind of soil. The gospel message, though it may seem small and weak, has the power to break through any human heart – if only we will listen and act on what we hear.

There may be areas of your heart you think are impenetrable, unreachable and unchangeable. There may be self-image problems, battles with addiction or alienation or abuse. You may feel trapped by all kinds of darkness inside you, things you feel you can't even admit. Let this parable give you hope. As you can see, there's a lot of power packed into that seed.

📻 *Ask a leader (maybe the same one) to give a three-minute testimony at this point about the power and impact of God's word in their lives.*

And let this parable make you treasure the word of God, the seed that is sown. The gospel message tells us that Jesus Christ has fully paid the price for sin on the cross, so the way is now open for us to know God and enjoy him forever, if only we will hear, accept and trust him.

But that is not a passive thing. It's not something that will just happen regardless of whether or not we choose to act on what we hear. The thief wants the seed of God's word to come to nothing in your life. Beware of the thief. Know his tactics. Recognize his activity. *"Thieves operate in this area. You are not obliged to be their victim. Guard your valuables!"*

And as you hear God's word today, will you accept it, welcome it, treasure it?

DAY AWAY 2: JAMES AND JOHN

Ask humbly

⊞ *Deliver Day Away Talk 2 using the notes below. The notes for this talk can also be downloaded from **www.ceministries.org** to enable you to adapt them for your group and add your own illustrations. Alternatively you could show Episode 8 (James and John) from the* Christianity Explored *DVD if this would be appropriate for your group.*

⊞ *There is a bulleted talk outline on page 52 of the group member's Handbook. Encourage people to write notes next to this outline as they listen to the talk.*

Aim

▦ To show the contrast between what James and John asked Jesus to do for them, and what Bartimaeus asked for.

▦ To show that following Jesus is about service, not status – and that we need to ask Jesus for mercy, not a reward.

▦ To challenge group members to consider what they want Jesus to do for them.

Introduction

In day-to-day life there are many situations where people ask us what we want them to do for us. In a shop we get asked: "Can I help you?" A care assistant visiting someone at home may ask: "What do you want me to do today?" If we visit the doctor, he or she may say: "What can I help you with?" At a burger bar it might just be: "Whaddya want?"

⊞ *Change the above examples as needed to suit your own situation.*

These people are all asking the same question: "What do you want me to do for you?"

But what if God asked you that question? If God said: "What do you want me to do for you?", what would you ask for? What would be your priority? The thing you most wanted?

In Mark chapter 10 Jesus asks that question twice: "What do you want me to do for you?" The answers he receives will help us to think about our own reply to this question.

The brothers...

James and John were brothers who were two of Jesus' closest disciples. They had spent three years with Jesus and knew him well. They had heard his amazing teaching; seen his power and authority over sickness, nature and even death; and watched him drive out evil spirits.

And they were there when Peter finally saw that Jesus was the Christ, God's only chosen King. They'd been given a unique opportunity to recognize Jesus' identity and understand his mission.

James and John had already heard Jesus say that he was going to suffer and die. In Mark 10 he explains that to them again.

👁 **Read Mark 10:33-34**

This is the third time that Jesus told his disciples what was going to happen. He knew that he was going to be betrayed, that he would suffer and die, and then rise again. He was on his way to Jerusalem, where the religious leaders and the Gentile Roman authorities would work together to have him killed.

This was why Jesus had come: *"to give his life as a ransom for many"* (Mark 10:45). He is telling his disciples what he is going to do for them, and what it will cost him – he will be mocked, spat upon, flogged and killed.

So how do James and John respond to this news? The next verse tells us.

👁 **Read Mark 10:35**

Jesus has just told James and John what he is going to do for them – and their response is to think about *themselves*. They want Jesus to do something just for them. And they even want him to agree before he knows what it is – *"we want you to do for us whatever we ask,"* they say.

...who asked for the wrong thing

So what did they want Jesus to do?

👁 **Read Mark 10:36-37**

James and John weren't asking for a small favour. They had grasped that Jesus was going to be exalted in some way, so they wanted the two most important positions in his kingdom – to sit on his right and left in places of power and prestige.

This was shockingly inappropriate. Their request is like being at a wedding and asking to be in all the photos, standing between the bride and groom!

Even though Jesus had explained his mission to them – that he was going to suffer and die – they are seeing his kingship in terms of power. And they want a share of it for themselves. A few days earlier the disciples had been arguing about which of them was the greatest. If James and John were given the two most important positions beside Jesus, it would settle that dispute once and for all.

They knew Jesus well – they knew what he said he had come to do – but they asked for the wrong thing.

As he had done so often before, Jesus used their question as an opportunity to teach them – about themselves, and also about himself and his mission. He started with a question of his own:

👁 **Read Mark 10:38-39a**

What does Jesus mean by "drink the cup I drink"? He means suffering God's anger for our sin as he dies as a ransom for many. Can James and John do what Jesus is about to do? Can they die to save sinners? Can they bring down the barrier separating sinful human beings from their Creator? Can they be raised to life again to prove that death and sin have been conquered?

"We can", they say. But clearly they cannot. They can't save others – they need to be saved from their own sinful rebellion against God. As Jesus said, they don't know what they're asking.

James and John want glory, but have no clue about the path of suffering that will lead Jesus to glory. It is a path that he is clearly willing to take. He knows it is only through his death and resurrection that they can be rescued from the results of their own sin, and enjoy a right relationship with Jesus for ever.

James and John want power and prestige, but Jesus offers something far more valuable – himself. As the brothers think about what they can gain for themselves, Jesus is thinking of what it will cost him as he serves and gives his life as a ransom for many.

Jesus then went on to show all the disciples that following him is about service, not status.

👁 Read Mark 10:41-44

It's not surprising that the other ten disciples were "indignant" with James and John. But their reaction shows that they, too, were concerned about status. They clearly didn't want James and John to be more important than the rest of them. But this isn't how Jesus wants them to think. He wants them to focus on what they can give, not what they can get.

Jesus reminds them of how most people operate:

> "You know that those who are regarded as rulers of the Gentiles lord it
> over them, and their high officials exercise authority over them"
> (Mark 10:41).

That sounds familiar, doesn't it? We've probably all experienced people in authority who use it as an opportunity to lord it over other people.

🔲 *Give a personal illustration here, maybe from a local situation or recent news item, of someone using their position of authority for personal gain or prestige.*

We're very used to people wanting to be seen as the greatest or pushing to get what they want, using other people as rungs on the ladder to be climbed on, or even just jumping to the front of a queue. It is easy to be impressed by that kind of eagerness to get ahead. But Jesus uses this as a contrast to how his followers should be. Their focus shouldn't be status, but service.

In other words, they shouldn't model themselves on what the rest of the world does. Their model is Jesus himself.

👁 Read Mark 10:45

Jesus is the supreme example of what he is calling his disciples to do. Jesus does have power and authority. He is the Son of God. But he hasn't come to be served, although that would be his right. Instead, he has come to be a servant – to serve others by dying for them, giving his life *"as a ransom for many"*. This is why you will sometimes hear Christians call Jesus the "servant King".

Actually that hunger for personal greatness and glory that sets us above our peers can never be satisfied. A glance at the lives of those who have pursued it shows that it is an impossible dream. They are never secure, and continue wanting more power, more prestige, more status. That's the way of the world – no matter how much we get we're never satisfied. We just want more.

⊞ Include an example here of a celebrity who has achieved success, fame and money – but found that it doesn't satisfy.

And there's a reason for that. We can only be fully satisfied by loving and serving the one who made us. It's the way he made us to be. We look for contentment, satisfaction and fulfilment in the wrong places. We look to wealth, or success, or family, or security, or sex, or power to fulfil our lives.

We make these things more important than God. The Bible calls this idolatry: turning something God has created into a substitute for God.

So we've seen what happened when Jesus asked James and John: *"What do you want me to do for you?"* They knew him well – but asked for the wrong thing. And Jesus then used this as an opportunity to teach them what it really means to follow him: that he came to serve, and that true greatness is not found in status but in service.

Later on, Jesus asks someone else the same question: *"What do you want me to do for you?"* But this man was very different from James and John.

The blind man...

Jesus and his disciples are still on their way to Jerusalem. When they reach Jericho, a large crowd joins them. And as they leave the city, they walk past a blind man who is sitting by the side of the road, begging. We don't know if this man had met Jesus before – probably not – but he knew who Jesus was.

👁 **Read Mark 10:46-47**

Bartimaeus couldn't see – and yet he was seeing clearly. He could see who Jesus was. This is the only time in Mark's Gospel that Jesus is called *"Son of David"*. Bartimaeus was right that Jesus belonged to the family line of King David, the greatest king the Israelites ever had. But "Son of David" means more than that.

God had made a promise to David that someone from his family would be king for ever. This would be God's only chosen King, the Christ or Messiah. When this blind man calls Jesus "Son of David", he is seeing that Jesus is God's promised King.

Jesus called Bartimaeus to him, and asked him the same question he had asked James and John: *"What do you want me to do for you?"* This time the answer was very different.

...who asked for the right thing

👁 **Read Mark 10:48-51**

Bartimaeus was a beggar. The only thing of value he had was his cloak. But when Jesus called him, he threw his cloak aside and rushed to Jesus. He had already asked Jesus for mercy. Now he very simply asks for what he needs – he wants to see.

This man knew that he had nothing to offer Jesus. He knew that he was helpless and hopeless. All he could do was come to God's King and beg for mercy. That means he knew he had no claim to it – it was undeserved and unmerited. How unlike James and John he was.

James and John had looked for glory. But Bartimaeus asked for mercy – and he received it.

👁 **Read Mark 10:52**

Jesus gave Bartimaeus what he asked for. He could already see who Jesus was. Now he could see Jesus with his own eyes. He had received the mercy he asked for – and his response was to follow Jesus.

Think of all the things that Bartimaeus could have done for the first time in his life, now that he had his sight. But of all the people he could now see, and all the possibilities life now held for him, he chooses to follow Jesus along the road. It's clear that for Bartimaeus Jesus was the ultimate treasure.

If you see who Jesus is, and experience his grace and mercy, following him will not be a boring, self-sacrificial chore. It will be the source of your greatest and lasting joy.

We're not told how the disciples reacted to this miracle. But James and John must have recognized the question Jesus asked Bartimaeus, the very same one he had asked them: *"What do you want me to do for you?"* And they would have seen the very different result.

They had come looking for status – and instead were shown the need to be servants. Bartimaeus came asking only for mercy – and received it.

It's a question for us to think about too. If Jesus asked you, "What do you want me to do for you?", what would you ask for?

DAY AWAY 3: HEROD

Choose wisely

*Deliver Day Away Talk 3 using the notes below. The notes for this talk can also be downloaded from **www.ceministries.org** to enable you to adapt them for your group and add your own illustrations. Alternatively you could show Episode 9 (Herod) from the* Christianity Explored *DVD if this would be appropriate for your group.*

There is a bulleted talk outline on page 54 of the group member's Handbook. Encourage people to write notes next to this outline as they listen to the talk.

Aim

To explain that ignoring Jesus' call to repent and believe will eventually earn us the rejection of Jesus.

To show from Herod's example that "we are the choices we have made".

To challenge group members not to put off the choice to follow Jesus.

Introduction

Have you ever looked back on one of those "fork in the road" moments in life, and wished you had taken the other path, the alternative course of action? It may have been something small, like buying a used car that broke down all the time – or a much larger decision, such as moving to another country for a job, then losing your job a month later.

If possible, include a personal example here of a choice you, or someone you know, made and then regretted.

As the old saying goes: "We are the choices we have made." In Mark chapter 6 we are told the harrowing story of a man who, it seems, would have given almost anything to undo the terrible situation his choices had got him into. He was a king – but he was played like a pawn.

👁 **Read Mark 6:17-29**

1. Herod's happiness

If we had lived in first-century Israel, at the same time as Herod, we would have said that Herod had it made. He was the king. He lived in a palace. And his birthday guest list read like a "who's who" of the great and the powerful (verse 21b).

Everything that could have brought him happiness was at his disposal, and what was not his he took – even his brother's wife, Herodias. Herod denied himself nothing in pursuit of his happiness. If he wanted Herodias, he got her.

So there he was – guest of honour at his own birthday, with a dancing girl, the daughter of Herodias, to entertain him.

👁 **Read Mark 6:22a**

It wasn't her skill as a ballerina that pleased the men. No, this was a seductive dance, and as Herod and his guests leered over the girl, he mixed his pleasure with a display of power.

👁 **Read Mark 6:22b-23**

Herod is making it clear that he has the power to give the girl anything she wants. The emphasis is on the *"ask me"*. He is showing his guests how red-blooded he is; how much he appreciates this entertainment, and how much he can afford to give away in his pursuit of happiness.

But this isn't just any dancer – she is the daughter of Herodias. And when the girl asks her mum what she should request from Herod, Herodias doesn't need to think twice. She is ready with her answer.

👁 **Read Mark 6:24**

Meanwhile, back in the banqueting room, and before the girl returns with her grisly request, King Herod is enjoying the revelry, and has forgotten about the trouble he is having...

2. Herod's problems

Happiness came at a price for Herod. Presumably he and his brother Philip weren't that close these days. And even the prized Herodias was causing Herod trouble.

👁 **Read Mark 6:17-20a**

This is the same John we read about in Mark chapter 1, who was telling people they needed to repent, and preparing them for the coming of Jesus. There was no one to whom John would not speak - even an adulterous king.

Herodias did not like the influence that John was having on Herod. She thought John was so inflexible in his views, so intolerant, so judgemental that she wanted him dead. And she made no secret of her willingness to assist in that process.

The nightmare for Herod was that she might succeed. That is why he kept them as far apart as possible. Herod was king – but actually in this central area of his life he was out of control.

He couldn't control himself, and he couldn't control his wife. All he could do was keep John out of her way, in prison. He didn't want to tell John to get out of town completely because he enjoyed listening to him.

So there was Herod being pulled apart by these two competing influences in his life. They couldn't happily exist together. Herodias and John knew that. But Herod desperately tried to find a way to have both.

He wanted to hear the word of God from John, but he also wanted to disobey the word of God with Herodias. He was being pulled apart by this conflict.

3. Herod liked to listen

In one sense Herod didn't like what John had to say any more than Herodias did. But while everyone else would say anything to ingratiate themselves with Herod, John told him the absolute truth.

👁 **Read Mark 6:18**

During *Christianity Explored*, you will have heard some things that are hard to take – about your sin, and God's anger, and the need to repent and believe. There are aspects of the gospel message that are hard to tell people. But we hope you can see that we care enough to tell you the truth. We want to be for you what John was to Herod.

Herod respected John for that, and he knew John was the real thing. This was the fork in the road for Herod. This was the moment he would look back on and perhaps long to return to.

Herod knew that John was a *"righteous and holy man"* (verse 20). He liked to listen to John. He was quite willing to hear him. But if he knew John was God's man, and that what he was saying was true – why didn't he act on it? Why wouldn't he repent?

4. Herod chose not to act

Why didn't Herod act decisively? What was stopping him? The answer is in the parable of the soils.

👁 **Read Mark 4:18-19**

That explains Herod. He heard God's word from John, but that word was being choked because Herod was worried about all the *"good things"* he was going to have to give up!

This is exactly the point you may be at in exploring the Christian faith. You may have reached that fork in the road. You may have seen the reality of your sin and where it will take you. You may have been thrilled to hear of the death of Jesus on the cross for sinners, and heard his call to follow him.

And you know you need to act on this – but the life-giving, life-changing seed of God's word is in danger of being stolen right now because you are thinking about what you would need to give up. You know that living with Jesus as Lord will mean changing or giving up parts of your life that you treasure.

In reality no one gives up anything good to follow Jesus. Those who trust him discover that knowing him is more valuable and satisfying than anything else.

But right now you may be admiring your beautiful thorns. If so, let Herod's experience inform yours...

5. Herod's distress

Back in the banqueting hall, Herod was making merry and probably forgot the battle that was raging within him.

His guests must have been longing to hear what the dancer was going to ask the king for – and perhaps they were calculating the loss to Herod's personal fortune if she did ask for half his kingdom.

They didn't have long to wait.

👁 Read Mark 6:25

Let's press the pause button there before this sinks in with Herod, and we'll give Herodias her moment.

There are people in the world who realise how powerful God's word is, and hate it so much that they will give anything to stop it having its impact on others. Herodias was like that.

This was a golden opportunity for Herodias and her daughter to have some financial independence. She could have become a very wealthy woman in seconds. But instead she trades half the kingdom for the perverse joy of silencing God's word in her husband's life.

We must see again the trouble Satan will go to in order to steal God's word. That should make you want to guard it and treasure it and accept it.

Herodias' daughter delivered her lines and revealed her request. It must have been a horrific moment for Herod as he instantly sobered up. He is the most powerful man in the room and in the kingdom. But as everyone laughed and cheered at the girl's obscene request, the king knew deep down he was a pawn.

You have probably heard of people talking about a life-changing moment when their whole life passed before their eyes. Surely this was one such moment for Herod. What a fool he had been. He had fallen into a trap of his own making. He had hesitated and dithered. He had listened to John repeatedly and knew what he said was right. Opportunity had knocked on Herod's door again and again, but he hadn't taken it.

But in the time it had taken the servants to refill his glass, his wife had seized her opportunity when it came.

I wonder if Herod's guests thought their host had got off lightly. He could have lost a fortune – instead John the preacher was going to lose his head. Maybe it was no big deal to them. But Mark tells us that Herod was *greatly distressed*.

👁 Read Mark 6:26-28

The pressure to keep his foolish oath to friends, family and work colleagues meant that Herod caved in. He hadn't acted on what John said about Herodias. So in the end he felt forced to do something he didn't want to do – and had John killed. He allowed the head that warned him, the tongue that told him to repent and be rescued, to be literally cut off.

Much as he feared John, Herod feared his peers more. We may feel that we are very different from Herod, but this is a pressure we all face as we respond to the gospel message. We can just imagine what friends and colleagues, even family members, will say if they hear we are followers of Christ. Will we deny what we know is right because of what family will think, what business colleagues may do, or what friends will say? Or because we know it will mean changing much-loved habits?

Followers of Jesus will be misunderstood

Amazingly, Jesus himself knew first-hand what it felt like to be misunderstood and ridiculed – even by his own family. We'll leave Herod for a moment to go back to Mark chapter 3, where we read that Jesus' family...

> "...went to take charge of him, for they said, 'He is out of his mind'"
> (Mark 3:21).

But when his family arrive at the house where he is teaching, Jesus says something remarkable.

👁 Read Mark 3:32-35

It may be that you feel afraid of what it will cost you to follow Jesus. I hope Jesus' words here are a great comfort. He reminds us that if you take his words seriously, even if the people closest to you think you're out of your mind, there is a loving family of fellow believers who are there to support and encourage us. Whoever does God's will, whoever follows Jesus, is your brother and sister and mother.

But it goes even further than that. In Mark chapter 10, Jesus makes this amazing promise to all those who put their trust in him:

👁 Read Mark 10:29-30

Followers of Jesus will be blessed

Yes, there will be persecutions of one kind or another. But with them, Jesus promises extraordinary blessings, and extraordinary joy that will far outweigh any suffering we might face. We may feel that we are like Herod in fearing what others will think of us – and Jesus doesn't hide the fact that there will be a cost to following him. But he also promises a family of fellow believers to help and encourage us – and exceptional blessings and joy.

> ⮕ Ask a leader to give a brief testimony about some of the blessings and joy they have experienced as a follower of Jesus.

Herod is mentioned a final time in the Gospels. The Roman Governor, Pontius Pilate, sends Jesus to meet Herod, and in Luke chapter 23, Luke records what happened.

The meeting between Herod and Jesus is ominous, not because of what *is* said, but because of what is *not* said.

👁 **Read Luke 23:8-9**

Herod had thought he could listen to Jesus like he had listened to John, but it was too late.

You see, there does come a time, after repeatedly refusing to repent, when sadly there is no longer an opportunity to do so. It's easy to put it off, to say that we don't have the time, to think that we have too much to lose, or that there'll be a more convenient time in the future.

Of course, it's never easy to repent. But Herod's story reminds us that there is a cost when we refuse to listen to God's word. It also warns us that we may not get an opportunity later. Herod threw many questions at Jesus – but received no answer.

It is a tragedy that John the Baptist lost his life. And yet the tragedy of Herod himself is even greater. We are the choices we have made. When Herod failed to choose wisely, he lost something that was more precious even than life itself: the opportunity to repent.

Ignoring Jesus' call to repent and believe may earn us the approval of other people. But it will eventually earn us... the rejection of Jesus.

Maybe you want more time to think about Jesus and the gospel message. There is a lot to think through. But don't be like Herod. His story warns us of the danger of putting off until later what should be done now.

How Herod must have longed to go back to that fork in the road of his life. Perhaps that's the fork at which you stand today.

COME AND DIE

What does it mean to follow Jesus?

7

▸ *Deliver Talk 7 using the notes below. The notes for this talk can also be downloaded from **www.ceministries.org** to enable you to adapt them for your group and add your own illustrations. Alternatively you could show Episode 10 (Come and die) from the* Christianity Explored *DVD if this would be appropriate for your group.*

▸ *There is a bulleted talk outline on page 60 of the group member's Handbook. Encourage people to write notes next to this outline as they listen to the talk.*

Aim

▪ To recap Mark's teaching about the *identity*, *mission* and *call* of Jesus.

▪ To show that following Jesus means denying self, and taking up our cross.

▪ To give group members an opportunity to respond personally to the call of Jesus.

Introduction

Tonight brings us to the end of our short journey through *Christianity Explored*. Thank you for exploring Mark's Gospel with us.

It may be the end of the course, but I hope you will find that it's just the beginning of a life with Jesus. That will depend on how you respond to him.

During the course we've seen what Mark says about Jesus: his *identity* (who he is), his *mission* (why he came) and his *call* (what it means to follow him). The verses we'll look at now will remind us of these three things, and also challenge us to think about where we stand with Jesus personally.

🔲 *You may want to use a simple visual aid to help your group follow the talk:*

   🔳 *Identity: who Jesus is*

   🔳 *Mission: why Jesus came*

   🔳 *Call: what it means to follow Jesus*

   🔳 *So what now?*

Identity: who Jesus is

Sometimes we think we can see something clearly, when actually we're only seeing part of the picture.

🔳 *Illustration: Show the picture of the young/old woman (available as a free download from **www.ceministries.org/downloads**). Ask your group what they can see. Some may only see the young woman, or the old woman. Help them to see both, but don't spend too long on this. It's fine if one or more of the group still can't see both women in the picture.*

The disciples had spent three years with Jesus. They had seen his amazing power and authority – as a teacher; over nature, evil spirits and sickness; and over death itself. But even so, they were still asking themselves: "Who is this?" They were eyewitnesses of everything Jesus had said and done – but still blind to his *identity*. They were only seeing part of the picture.

If being with Jesus in person hadn't cured their blindness, what could? To help answer that question, Jesus healed a blind man – but it was a very unusual healing. This was the only time when Jesus didn't cure someone immediately.

👁 Read Mark 8:22-26

This man was healed in stages. He started totally blind; then was able to see a little, but not clearly; then finally his sight was completely restored. This gradual healing reflects the gradual growth of the disciples' understanding. To start with they couldn't see who Jesus was. They didn't know his *identity*. But in chapter 8 they began to see the truth – but not clearly.

Mark 8:27-29 focuses on the *identity* of Jesus. He asks his disciples firstly who people say he is – and then he asks them who *they* think he is:

👁 Read Mark 8:27-29

Who does the evidence say about who Jesus is? Who do you think Jesus is? You need to settle this issue for yourself because it could be a matter of life and death for you.

Peter gives an amazing answer. He has come to see that Jesus is not another prophet, or a great teacher or healer, but the Christ, the Messiah – the King God had promised to send, who has now come into the world.

So like the blind man, the disciples can now see who Jesus is. Or can they? They see his *identity* – that Jesus is the Christ, God's only chosen King. But their "sight" is not fully healed. Although they see who Jesus is, they don't yet see why he has come or what it means to follow him. They are only seeing part of the picture.

Mission: why Jesus came

As soon as the *identity* of Jesus is established, look what happens next. The focus turns to the *mission* of Jesus.

👁 Read Mark 8:30-32a

This is why Jesus has come – to suffer, be rejected, die and rise again – to *"give his life as a ransom for many"*. And Jesus confirms this *mission* repeatedly, as we've seen in previous sessions.

But now we'll read the whole of verse 32:

👁 Read Mark 8:32

Peter takes a lot on himself here as he rebukes the one he has just identified as God's promised King. But he doesn't get far. See verse 33:

"Having in mind the things of men" may have meant Peter had great hopes that his own importance would grow as a close ally of the King. Or he may have wanted King Jesus to free the Jewish people from the hated Romans who had occupied their country. But neither of these things could happen if Jesus was killed as he predicted.

Peter doesn't want Jesus to suffer and die because that wouldn't serve "the things of men". But Peter isn't the only one who doesn't want Jesus to die in this way. Jesus understands that *Satan* doesn't want him to fulfil "the things of God" either.

In trying to prevent Jesus from going through suffering, rejection and death, Peter was siding with Satan, not with God.

Our temptation will be much the same as Peter's at this point: to think of Jesus' death as something unpleasant, unnecessary – an embarrassment. But are we, like Peter, only seeing part of the picture?

Peter was blind to what the cross was about. Are we blind? Do we see it as a waste or a rescue?

As you think about the cross, are you thankful to Jesus for dying to pay for your sin so that you don't have to pay for it yourself?

Sadly, many people are impressed by Jesus, but the influence of Satan makes them fear the rejection they may suffer through being his follower, and so they walk away.

The influence of Satan is as strong as it is subtle. It results in a world where people will tolerate, endorse and even embrace almost every way of thinking and behaving. But to trust in the Lord Jesus Christ, who served me by giving his life on the cross to pay for my sin, so that I can be forgiven of my sin and put right with God for ever – that is perceived in every culture to be the most embarrassing belief there is!

It is amazing that it should be like this. Our Creator gave his life to rescue us from the terrible consequences of our rebellion against him. How could we be ashamed by that?

Yet for many, as for Peter, the *mission* of Jesus is too shameful to be associated with. The fear of friends and family, neighbours and colleagues laughing at our love and gratitude to Jesus has caused many to walk away from him, even though they are personally convinced that he is the real thing.

Satan failed to stop Jesus going to the cross. But he will still try to stop you from following the Christ of the cross. That is why Jesus makes it crystal clear both what it will mean to be his follower, and why we should *want* to be his followers...

Call: what it means to follow Jesus

We pick up where we left off and turn now to the *call* of Jesus in Mark 8:34-38.

👁 **Read Mark 8:34-38**

In verse 38 Jesus warns us what will happen if we are ashamed of him and his words. He explains that human thinking is instinctively unfaithful to God and rebellious against him. That means it's a very tough environment for those who choose to follow Jesus.

Listen again to what he says in verse 34:

> *"If anyone would come after me, he must deny himself and take up his cross and follow me."* (Mark 8:34)

That is exactly what Peter was struggling with. He had in mind the things of men – following a popular, powerful leader, being one of his top men, seeing him defeat their Roman enemies – that was what Peter wanted.

But Jesus says: "No! I have come to suffer, be rejected and die, and I will rise again so that I can rescue you. And if you are going to follow me, you must deny your right to run your own life – and just as this world rejects me, so it will reject you because you follow me."

It is as though Jesus says to Peter: "Not only is there no escape from the shame of the cross for me, Peter; there is no escape from the shame of the cross for you if you will be my disciple."

Just as the cross meant rejection, humiliation and suffering for Jesus, so it may mean the same for us as his followers.

Denying yourself means putting your desire for comfort and acceptance in this world to one side, so that it doesn't stop you from following Jesus and being saved. We all crave comfort and acceptance, and that's why Jesus says in verse 35:

> *"For whoever wants to save his life will lose it, but whoever loses his life for me and for the gospel will save it"* (Mark 8:35).

If you want the approval of this world and can't bear to think of being rejected by it, then you will save your life now, but lose it eternally.

But if you see the treasure that is in Jesus and choose to follow him, then even though the world may mock you and reject you now, your life will be saved, eternally. Jesus is the only one who has ever died and then risen to live for ever – so he is the only one who can make that a reality for us. If we want to save our lives, we must entrust them to Jesus.

Jesus emphasizes this point in the next verses:

> *"What good is it for a man to gain the whole world, yet forfeit his soul? Or what can a man give in exchange for his soul?"* (Mark 8:36-37)

The point is that we are not just flesh and blood. Your soul is the essential you – the part that can't be X-rayed or touched – the part of you that lasts eternally, either enjoying God for ever, or separated from his blessing for ever, in hell. Can you see how incomparably precious your soul is?

Your soul will last for ever, but Satan blinds us to the *eternal* realities. Instead, he gets us to think only about the temporary trinkets of this life.

Satan does something like this, but far worse. He's not worried about cream cakes or large stomachs! He wants us to forget about the future – and about our eternal soul – and to focus instead on the here and now.

But as Jesus said:

> *"What good is it for a man to gain the whole world, yet forfeit his soul?"* (Mark 8:36)

🔲 *In 1000 AD, 186 years after the death of Emperor Charlemagne, officials of the Emperor Otto re-opened Charlemagne's tomb.[3] Before them was an extraordinary sight. In the midst of all the finery buried with him – the gold, the jewels, the priceless treasure – there was the skeleton of Charlemagne himself, still seated on his throne, still wearing his crown.*

> *In his lap, there lay a Bible, and a bony finger rested on Mark chapter 8 verse 36: "What good is it for a man to gain the whole world, yet forfeit his soul?"*

Jesus has been very clear about the cost of following him. His disciples needed to know what it would mean – and so do we. But we also need to be clear about what Jesus is **not** saying.

Firstly, please don't think that the toughness of being a Christian *earns* us our salvation. That is the opposite of the gospel message. We have seen during the course that Jesus *"did not come to be served, but to serve, and give his life as a ransom for many"* (Mark 10:45). It is *Jesus* who earns our salvation, not *us*.

---

3   Charlemagne – King of the Franks (768–814), King of the Lombards (774–814) and Emperor (800–814); b. 2 April c. 742, d. 28 January 814. His tomb in Aix au Chapelle was opened by Otto III (b. July 980, d. 23 January 1002) in AD 1000.

And secondly, don't think that being a Christian is all about pain with nothing to gain. Jesus is very clear about the cost, but he also tells us that what is given up is nothing compared to what is gained. We read during our day away about the promises Jesus made to his followers:

👁 **Read Mark 10:29-30**

Do you see what Jesus says? Even those who leave the comforts of home, the support of family, the wealth of property and their normal means of support because of Jesus will not go without.

Jesus will see to it that they are comforted, supported and provided for. They will face persecution for standing up for Jesus and the gospel, but they will not be neglected by him. They will enjoy an unimaginable, unfading and unending quality of life, enjoying God for ever.

A true follower of Jesus is someone who clearly sees what it will cost to follow him – but does it joyfully anyway, knowing that Jesus is worth infinitely more.

📽 *Show the old/young woman picture again.*

For many people, when they look at this picture they only see one woman. They think they are seeing clearly, but in fact they're not seeing the whole picture. The same was true for the blind man. At first he couldn't see at all; then he could see something, but not clearly; and finally his blindness was cured and he could see clearly.

The gradual healing of the blind man reflects the gradual growth of the disciples' understanding. In Mark 8 they saw at last the *identity* of Jesus – that he is the Christ, God's only chosen King. But they didn't yet see the whole picture. So Jesus patiently explained his *mission* to them – that he must suffer, be rejected, die and rise again. And then he *called* them to follow him – by denying themselves and taking up their cross.

So what now?

I wonder whether you are like the disciples. Can you see the *identity* of Jesus? Can you see the necessity of his *mission*? Are you ready to respond to his *call*?

Or are you struggling with "The Week 7 Dilemma"?

📽 *Note: If you are not using* Christianity Explored *weekly, use another name such as "The Last Session Dilemma" or "The Mark 8 Dilemma".*

"The Week 7 dilemma" is a dilemma that you are likely to find yourself in having met Jesus in Mark. It is this:

On the one hand you may find that you are *intrigued or personally impressed* by Jesus, but on the other you worry that you will be *publicly embarrassed* by him.

You may have begun to feel this tension: you are intrigued or impressed by all that you have seen of Jesus – maybe his stature has grown in your eyes and you are amazed to see that he is the opposite to what you always thought.

But as you work out how you are going to respond to him, and if you will become his follower, there is that nagging question of how family, friends and colleagues will react to you trusting in Christ.

That's "The Week 7 Dilemma". If it's a dilemma you're struggling with, I'd love to help you think it through. I'm happy to talk with you after the session, or arrange another time when we could meet. Or you may find it helpful to keep exploring Christianity by coming to one of our regular small groups.

> 💬 *Note: Please adapt the suggestions above to fit your own situation. You may have a follow-on course that would be suitable, or a sermon series to recommend. Any one-to-one meetings with group members are best done by a leader of the same sex as the guest.*

As you work out how you will respond to Jesus, let me leave you with a greater question: how will he respond to you?

👁 Read Mark 8:38

On that day, when we see Jesus in unparalleled majesty, it will be unimaginable that any of us could ever have been ashamed of him.

But the greater wonder of that day will be this:

Those who have answered his call and followed Jesus will discover that, in spite of all the sin and rebellion of our lives, *he* will not be ashamed of us.

Conclusion

So - what do you see when you look at Jesus?

■ What do you see when you look at Jesus' *identity*? Is he just a good man, or is he the Christ, the Son of God?

■ What do you see when you look at Jesus' *mission*? Is his death a tragic waste, or is it a rescue – a "ransom for many"?

■ And what do you see when you look at Jesus' *call*? Is it a way of losing your life, or a way of gaining it?

Answering tough questions

OPEN TO QUESTION

One of the most important aspects of running a course like *Christianity Explored* is that it encourages guests to ask questions in an environment where they will be taken seriously, and not be ridiculed or belittled. You should encourage your group with words like: "No question is too simple, or too difficult – *Christianity Explored* is about you finding answers to the important questions of life".

It is this atmosphere of open enquiry that encourages people to "open up" about spiritual things, and to approach the Bible not as a dead textbook, but as the source for answers. It is your job to help create this environment by your openness, honesty and willingness to talk in a relaxed way about things that group members may find particularly difficult to articulate.

WHY PEOPLE DON'T ASK QUESTIONS

There are a number of reasons why people won't ask questions:

- **Because they don't have any!** Some guests may not have thought much about spiritual things. It may be they grew up in a Christian home, and didn't question the things they have always been taught. However, the word of God often provokes reactions and questions. So in the course of reading Mark, they are likely to come up with some. And if they are part of a larger group that is dealing with questions, then they will be encouraged to join in. Don't force the issue – let them develop in their own time.

- **Because they are frightened of appearing stupid.** This is a BIG issue for many people. If they think the question is simple, or that they will be belittled by others for asking it, then they will not speak up. The key here is to make sure you keep repeating the words: "No question is too simple, or too difficult – *Christianity Explored* is about you finding answers to the important questions of life".

- **Because they are shy.** Some people just aren't good at speaking up in groups. And that is fine. Just make sure that you are able to talk with them personally about their questions. Watch out for the tell-tale signs of a wrinkled forehead as they read or listen.

- **Because they need time.** Some people just need more time to get to the question. They may think of something later that evening or during the next week. So you should always give an opportunity to deal with questions from the previous session that have occurred to people, and don't make them feel that everyone is taking a step backwards because "all that was dealt with last time".

WHY DO PEOPLE ASK QUESTIONS?

It might seem obvious: "Because they want to know the answer" – but it often runs much deeper than that:

- **Because I want to test you.** The precise question they ask may not be of particular concern to them. It could just be that they have heard it expressed by others, or know that it is a tricky question for Christians to answer. What they are more interested in is how you handle it (*see below*). By not being rattled, and by taking the question seriously and demonstrating that you have given it some thought, you are answering "the question behind the question", which is: are these people trustworthy? Always take questions seriously.

- **Because I genuinely don't understand.** There may be a huge variation in Bible knowledge in your group, and some will want to ask what you might consider to be really basic questions: "Who was Jesus?", "When did all this happen?", "What is prayer?" etc. Again, treat them seriously, and make sure the rest of the group do not look down on those with less knowledge than they have.

- **Because I have had a distressing personal experience.** There is a world of difference between someone asking: "Why does God allow suffering?" as an academic question, and someone who asks the same question having watched a close relative die of cancer recently. The way you answer the two may be completely different. And of course, you will not know if others listening in to your answer are carrying a burden of disappointment or personal pain. Always answer compassionately.

- **Because I have been let down.** The way a question is phrased may be the key to getting an insight here. So instead of "What is prayer?", asking "Why does God answer some prayers and not others?" may indicate that the questioner has some specific disappointment in mind. Similarly, a question about Christians being hypocrites may relate to some bitter personal experience of a Christian or a church in the past. Always answer honestly.

■ **Because I want to be sure it all makes sense.** The interest in a particular question may not be because it is a problem, but rather that they are seeking a sense that the Christian faith as a whole sticks together coherently. So answering in a way that connects the question with the big picture of the Bible's message is important. Answer from the Bible, not just from sensible reasons or philosophy.

HOW DO I ANSWER?

The following two appendices give you some suggested approaches to answering the substance of the difficult questions that people ask. But, as we have suggested above, it is equally important that we answer in the right way. 1 Peter 3:15-16 says:

> "But in your hearts set apart Christ as Lord[1]. Always be prepared[2] to give an answer to everyone who asks you to give the reason[3] for the hope that you have. But do this with gentleness and respect.[4]"

Notice four things about giving answers:

1. **The person who answers the questions needs to be someone who is personally committed to the lordship of Christ.** This is important, because the answer to their unspoken questions is not your arguments or knowledge – it is your life. Many of their most important questions will remain unarticulated, like: "Is this relevant to me?", "What does this look like in a real person?" and "Could I be a Christian?" All these questions are answered by the way you live and model being a disciple and follower of Jesus. Are you displaying the joy, peace, love and contentment in life that comes from knowing Christ as Lord? If you come to *Christianity Explored* feeling resentful, angry and doubtful in your own standing with God, then you cannot hope to influence your group members for the gospel. They may hear convincing arguments from your mouth, but your life will speak much more loudly.

2. **You must be ready to answer.** Take time to think through the answers on the following pages, and come to your own conclusions about them. You should be as sure in your answer as the Bible is – no less, no more! For example, on the questions of the origin of evil, or the reason for suffering, we do not have final

and complete answers from the Bible, and therefore, we must be careful in what we say and acknowledge our difficulty with these issues, rather than insisting that we have it all sewn up.

3. **You must have a reasonable answer.** In other words, saying: "Just have faith in the Bible" is not enough – even if we cannot prove it with complete certainty, we have to show the reasonableness of our faith.

4. **You must answer gently and respectfully.** Even (perhaps especially) when people are hostile, we must model kindness, love and fairness in our attitudes, thinking and speaking. Only in this way will we win people for the gospel.

MORE TIPS ON ANSWERING QUESTIONS

- **Involve the group.** Resist the temptation to answer the question on your own. It is good practice to first ask: "Does anyone else find this a difficult question?" You can then address your answers to the whole group. It may also be that you have Christians in your group who will be able to help answer. So you might ask: "Has anyone in the group got an answer to that?" In this way you are also training and encouraging the Christians to get involved in the discussion. It has been the experience on many *Christianity Explored* courses that involving the group in answering questions often helps other "not-yet-Christians" start to see the wrong thinking in some of their doubts as they start to argue back with a questioner!

- **Go to the Bible.** The Bible is the sword of the Spirit, so we must have confidence that if we direct people to its answers, God will do his work through it. If you can, go to a Bible passage to read and then explain, especially if it is in Mark's Gospel.

- **Empathize.** Don't give the impression that you have everything figured out. If you have wrestled with this question in the past – tell them. If you still have areas that you wrestle with, say so, but also tell them why it is no longer a problem in the larger scheme of your faith. For example: "I find suffering (eg: a natural disaster such as a major earthquake) very difficult to understand, but I know that God weeps over it too and cares, because he sent Jesus into the world, and he has experienced the pain and suffering of our broken world."

- **Give them time.** Don't assume that they will sort out everything right at that moment. Many of the ideas and arguments and thoughts from the Bible will take time to sink in and be processed. Leave the question open for another day, and encourage them to think about it seriously over the next week, eg: "There are some big things to think about there, and you might not feel this discussion has answered all your questions immediately, but can I ask you to think about it, and maybe we can return to it next time if you want to go into it in more depth."

And finally...

Don't be afraid to admit that you don't know the answer to a question. But do promise to find out before the next session.

You will find help in answering questions in the next two appendices (starting on pages 237 and 245). In addition, **www.christianityexplored.org** includes video clips giving answers to popular questions.

Two *Christianity Explored* websites to help you:

www.christianityexplored.org
For non-Christians whether or not they're on a course

www.ceministries.org
For leaders looking for information, downloads and resources

Questions from Mark's Gospel

MARK 1:2-3

What are these strange quotes at the start?

Mark quotes from the Jewish Bible (what we call the Old Testament) – Malachi 3:1, and Isaiah 40:3 (written 700 years before Jesus was born). They are quotes from passages that promise a messenger who will announce the arrival of a rescuer King – the Christ or Messiah, who will save God's people from judgment. The promise of a messenger is clearly fulfilled by John the Baptist in Mark 1:4-8. Even his clothing (Mark 1:6) was like that of an Old Testament prophet, in particular Elijah (2 Kings 1:8).

MARK 1:13

What are angels?

The word literally means "messenger". They are spiritual beings in the service of God, who particularly are sent to deliver messages. An angel delivers the wonderful message of the resurrection in Mark 16:5-6. He is described as looking like a young man dressed in a white robe. No mention of wings!

MARK 1:23-27

What are evil spirits and demons?

The Bible says that there is an unseen spiritual world, which includes angels and evil spirits. According to the Bible, Satan, or the devil, is a fallen angel who is in rebellion against God and hostile to God's people. Demons are part of that fallen spiritual world, and serve Satan. Although Satan and his demons are powerful, the New Testament shows that Jesus has overcome Satan by the power of his death on the cross (see Colossians 2:15).

Note: If this topic comes up, deal with it briefly but don't allow it to dominate the session – some people are fascinated by "the dark side" and want to talk about it for hours. And make sure you explain to them that Christians have nothing to fear from the devil – Jesus has defeated him.

MARK 1:34; 7:36

Why did Jesus tell the people he healed not to tell anyone?

No one has ever healed people as Jesus did. It was instantaneous, spectacular and complete. People didn't just "start to feel a bit better". They were completely better immediately. Not surprisingly Jesus drew huge crowds who wanted to see these amazing miracles, but who seemed less interested in his teaching. Jesus did not want people coming just to see signs and wonders. He rejected such people (Mark 8:11-13). In Mark 1:45 it becomes clear that he has to leave the crowds in order to teach. He probably told people not to tell anyone so that the crowds would not become a problem.

MARK 2:10

Why did Jesus call himself the Son of Man?

"Son of man" is a Jewish term meaning simply "a man". But "Son of Man" is also a well-known title used in the Old Testament for the Messiah – God's promised King. See Daniel 7:13-14. The religious leaders would have understood that when Jesus used the title "Son of Man", it was a claim to be the Messiah.

MARK 2:16

What is a Pharisee?

This group of strict Jews did not just obey the Old Testament but held to many strict traditions. They were seen as some of the most holy men in Israel. But Jesus called them "hypocrites", which literally means "play-actors", because of the way they showed off their religion and self-righteousness. He strongly condemns them in passages such as Mark 7:6-9.

MARK 2:19

Who is the "bridegroom"?

Jesus is making the point that, for the disciples, fasting (going without food) is totally inappropriate when he's with them, just as it would be for wedding guests to be miserable at a wedding. Jesus is saying he is the bridegroom of God's people. This is another claim to be the Messiah promised in the Old Testament (Isaiah 54:5; 62:4-5; Hosea 2:16-20).

MARK 2:21-22

What is the new cloth/old coat, new wine/old skins story about?

People complained that Jesus was not following the religious rules of his day (Mark 2:18). Jesus says that the faith he has come to bring is not about rules at all. Jesus cannot be "fitted into" their "religion of rules". He came to bring a living friendship with God, not rules. Jesus brings grace, love and peace – not religious rules.

MARK 2:23

What is the Sabbath?

The Sabbath was the special day of rest when no work was done. The Sabbath was an opportunity for God's people to remember God's creation and how he rescued them from Egypt.

MARK 3:6

Who are the Herodians?

These were supporters of Herod Antipas, the king of Judea, who depended on the controlling Roman Empire for his power. They would have seen Jesus as a threat to Herod's rule.

MARK 3:13-19

Why did Jesus choose twelve apostles?

Jesus calls the twelve apostles on a mountainside. In the Old Testament God shows himself to his people on mountains (eg: Genesis 8; Exodus 19; and 1 Kings 18). There were twelve tribes of Israel – God's people in the Old Testament. Jesus is making the point that God is calling a new group of people to follow him.

MARK 3:22

What does it mean to be possessed by Beelzebul?

Beelzebul is another name for the devil. Note that the religious authorities don't question whether Jesus is powerful or whether the miracles happen. They simply ask where his power comes from. They say that Jesus is possessed by the devil and is driving out demons. Jesus replies that their claim is foolish – after all, if the "prince of demons" really was driving out other demons, then he would be fighting against himself.

MARK 3:29

What is the blasphemy against the Holy Spirit that will never be forgiven?

The religious leaders have seen Jesus perform wonderful miracles, and have heard his astonishing teaching. Now they claim that the work of the Holy Spirit is actually the work of the devil. Jesus' warning has nothing to do with swearing at the Holy Spirit – in simple terms, it means rejecting the only way of forgiveness that God has provided. Of course, this sin is only unforgivable for as long as a person goes on committing it. Many of the same religious leaders changed their minds about Jesus later, and so were forgiven (Acts 6:7). This is vital to understand. There can be no forgiveness if we reject Jesus.

MARK 4:2

Why did Jesus teach in parables?

Jesus told these memorable stories to teach spiritual truths. Parables have a clear surface meaning, but also a deeper meaning (often just one main point), which Jesus explains to those who will listen (Mark 4:1-34). There is a spiritual principle here: "To everyone who has, more will be given" (Luke 19:26). The disciples are intrigued by the parables and draw nearer to Jesus to hear the explanation. But, to the crowd, the parables are just curious stories. They hear, but do not understand (Mark 4:12). All people are like moths or bats reacting to light. They are either attracted to Jesus' teaching, or repelled by it.

MARK 4:40

Why does Jesus say: "Do you still have no faith?"

Despite all the evidence they've seen, the disciples still don't have faith in Jesus (note: to "have faith" in someone means to trust him or her). The disciples express terror rather than trust both before and after Jesus acts. Interestingly, just before this miracle, Jesus has told three parables making the point that God's word is powerful. He then calms the storm with a word. The disciples should have drawn the obvious conclusion.

MARK 6:3

Did Jesus have brothers and sisters?

These were the natural children of Joseph and Mary, conceived after the birth of Jesus. See also Mark 3:32. This answers the question as to whether Mary remained a virgin after the birth of Jesus. In addition, Matthew 1:25 certainly implies that Joseph and Mary had a normal sexual relationship after Jesus was born.

MARK 6:7-11

Why did Jesus send out the twelve disciples?

Jesus sends out the twelve disciples, telling them to expect some to accept and some to reject their message. They are to reject those who, by refusing to listen, reject them. The reference to shaking

239

off dust refers to what Jews did on returning to Israel from Gentile countries, which they viewed as "unclean". For the disciples to do it in a Jewish village was like calling the village Gentile! It is a mark of judgment (see also Acts 13:51).

MARK 6:14-29

Why is there all this stuff about John the Baptist?

Mark tells us about the death of John the Baptist to make an important point. It answers the question that is implied in Mark 6:1-13: why don't people see who Jesus is? The answer is that people reject Jesus because, like Herod, they will not repent. In other words, they will not turn from their rebellion against God.

MARK 7:24-30

Why does Jesus call this woman a dog?

Mark tells us this incident to show that Jesus has come to rescue and save Gentiles as well as Jews. The woman is a Gentile (= non Jew) from near the city of Tyre. "Children" here refers to the Jews, and "dogs" was a common, unflattering expression that Jews used for any Gentile person. So Jesus is saying: "It isn't right to take what belongs to the Jews and give it to you Gentiles." In her reply (v 28) the woman is saying; "Yes Lord – I acknowledge that as a Gentile woman I have no right to ask help from you, the Jewish Messiah. But you have such great power and mercy that you must have enough to help me as well!" Jesus is impressed by her faith and her persistence, and grants her request.

MARK 8:15

What is the yeast of the Pharisees and Herod?

Yeast – the stuff you put in bread to make it rise – is used as a picture in the New Testament to refer to the influence of someone or something. Just as a tiny amount of yeast has a great effect on the whole batch of dough, so Jesus warns against being affected by the sinful attitudes of the Pharisees and Herod: specifically, these would be hypocrisy and worldliness.

MARK 8:17-21

Why do the disciples not understand?

Jesus has fed thousands in the desert (twice), healed people, forgiven sin, cast out evil spirits and stilled storms with a word. So what's wrong with the disciples? As the following two stories show – they need spiritual help to understand the truth that is staring them in the face. Spiritual truth can only be revealed by God's Spirit.

MARK 8:22-25

Why is there a two-part healing?

Jesus hasn't lost his touch, or found it difficult to heal this man. He is doing the healing as a kind of "acted parable", to explain what happens next. When Peter announces that Jesus is "the Messiah" in Mark 8:29, he is like the man in Mark 8:24 (he has partial sight). It is clear from the verses that follow – where Peter rebukes Jesus – that although he has understood *who* Jesus is, he has not yet realized *why* Jesus has come (Mark 8:30-33).

Why does Jesus say: "Get behind me, Satan!"?

Peter had recognized that Jesus was the Christ, but he could not understand why Jesus had to suffer and die. Jesus recognizes in Peter's words a temptation to reject God's plan that the Christ should die on the cross. It is not that Peter is Satan, or that Satan has "taken control". It is just that Peter is saying what the devil wants, which is to knock Jesus off course in his mission to rescue us by dying on the cross and rising to life again.

What does Jesus mean when he says that some "will not taste death before they see that the kingdom of God has come with power"?

This probably refers to the transfiguration of Jesus, recorded immediately after (Mark 9:2-7), although it could also be a reference to the coming of the Holy Spirit on the Day of Pentecost (Acts 1:8).

Who are Elijah and Moses?

Both of these people represent the Old Testament: Moses was the law-giver and Elijah the greatest of the Old Testament prophets. The fact that they talk with Jesus shows that he is the one the Old Testament is pointing to.

What does Jesus mean when he says: "Elijah does come first"?

The disciples have failed to recognize that John the Baptist was the Elijah-like messenger promised in Malachi 4:5-6 who would come before "the Lord". Elijah was a prophet in the eighth century BC who lived out in the wilderness, wearing animal skins and a leather belt (2 Kings 1:8). This is how John the Baptist is described in Mark 1:6. Jesus makes it clear that John was the fulfilment of the prophecy concerning Elijah.

Why does Jesus tell us to cut our hands off?

Jesus obviously did not intend that a Christian should physically cut off a hand or foot, or pluck out an eye. It's not as if sin is confined to a particular part of our bodies. Jesus is exaggerating to make a point: "If anything is stopping you from entering the kingdom of God, it is better to take drastic action to rid yourself of it, whatever it is, than to end up in hell for ever." The most important thing is getting right with God. The logic is clear: temporary pain is better than eternal punishment.

MARK 10:1-12

What does Jesus think about divorce?
Jesus makes it clear that divorce is always against the perfect purpose of God. God's plan in creation is that married people should live together for their whole lives (see Genesis 2:24). Jesus says that if people seek a divorce because they have found an alternative partner, such action is adultery (Mark 10:11-12). It is only because people's hearts are so hard (Mark 10:5) that divorce could ever be permitted. The danger is either that we use the concession of verse 5 as an excuse for deliberate sin, or that we think that divorce cuts us off from God for ever. Christ came to die for all sin, including the failures of divorce.

Note: Be aware that you are likely to have people in your group who have experienced the reality of broken marriages. For some this may be a significant personal issue.

MARK 10:15

What does it mean to "receive the kingdom of God like a little child"?
The disciples need to understand that they have nothing to offer God, and must therefore depend fully on God, just as a little child depends fully on its parents. Jesus is not implying that children are innocent or pure – neither of which are traits of most children!

MARK 10:38

What did Jesus mean when he said: "Can you drink the cup I drink"?
In the Old Testament, "the cup" was generally a reference to suffering. It also refers to the cup of God's anger (see Jeremiah 25:15-16). In Mark 10:38, Jesus is showing that the disciples don't know what they are talking about. They, unlike Jesus, have their own sin to deal with and therefore cannot suffer God's wrath on other people's behalf; a sinless substitute is required. However, Jesus adds – in verse 39 – that they will suffer.

MARK 11:12-14, 20-21

Why did Jesus curse the fig-tree?
This can seem strange as it is Jesus' only destructive miracle. Mark interweaves the cursing of the fig-tree with the events in the temple (Mark 11:15-19, 27-33). In the same way that Jesus curses the fig-tree for having no fruit on it, he condemns the "fruitlessness" of Israel's religion (ie: the lack of genuine worship, the failure to recognize Jesus as the Messiah, etc).

MARK 12:1

What does the story about the vineyard mean?
The vineyard was a common Old Testament symbol of Israel. In particular, this passage is very similar to Isaiah 5, where the people of Israel are rebuked for the terrible way they have rejected God, and are told that God's righteous judgment will come. Jesus' hearers would have understood that the "man" in the parable was God, that the "vineyard" was the people of God, and that the missing fruit was loyalty to the son (= Jesus).

MARK 12:10

What is a capstone?
This is the most important stone; the foundation stone. Here it means that

although Israel's leaders have rejected Jesus, he is still the Messiah, and will become the Saviour through dying on the cross.

MARK 12:18-27

What's the point of the strange "one bride for seven brothers" story?

In Jesus' day there were two major religious groups who argued about what happens after we die. The Pharisees believed in life after death. The Sadducees said that death was the end. So the Sadducees came up with this question to trick Jesus. In his answer, Jesus makes two things very clear. **First**, that there is life beyond the grave. He says that the Bible refers to God as "the God of Abraham, the God of Isaac and the God of Jacob". It must mean that Abraham, Isaac and Jacob are still alive. God is the God of the living, not the dead. But **second**, Jesus makes it clear that we must not think of life after death as though it was the same as this life, but without some of the bad bits. It will be completely different. So different that our relationships will all change. We will recognize and know our close friends in the world to come – but it is a mistake to think that things like marriage will be the same.

MARK 13:14

What is "the abomination that causes desolation"?

This is an example where a passage in another Gospel helps. Luke 21:20 substitutes the words "Jerusalem being surrounded by armies", for this phrase. It refers to the occasion in AD 65 when Roman armies surrounded Jerusalem after a political uprising. After a horrific five-year war, the Roman armies entered the city, desecrated the temple, and then proceeded to pull it down and destroy the city. Jesus' words in Mark 13 came true.

MARK 13:32

Why does Jesus not know the date of his own return?

Some suggest that Jesus could not be perfect, or God, if he does not know this important fact. When Jesus was born as a man he "emptied himself" (Philippians 2:7, NASB). As a child, Jesus had to grow in wisdom, just as all human children do. He was not born with complete knowledge built in. This is one of those things which helps to verify the trustworthiness of biblical history. If someone was making up the story of Jesus Christ, he would never have left in Mark 13:32!

MARK 14:12

What are "the Festival of Unleavened Bread" and "the Passover lamb"?

God commanded the Israelites to keep the annual feasts of Passover and Unleavened Bread to remind them of how he had rescued them from slavery in Egypt (Exodus 12:14-20). Israel could only be saved from the tenth plague, the death of the firstborn, by killing a lamb, eating its roasted flesh with bitter herbs and unleavened bread, and smearing the blood on the door frames. Wherever there was blood on a door, the Lord "passed over" the house and spared the firstborn (Exodus 12:1-13). The meal eaten in Mark 14:12-26 takes place at Passover. Jesus' death would be the true means of rescue from God's judgment; it would be the true Passover. This is why Jesus is sometimes referred to as the Lamb of God.

What is the "blood of the covenant"?

Passover commemorates rescue from slavery in Egypt, and from the wrath of God, by the pouring out of blood (Exodus 12:23). That rescue was followed by a covenant (an agreement made by God on behalf of his people) that was sealed by a blood sacrifice (Exodus 24:6). Jesus' sacrificial death mirrors this. He bled and died to turn God's wrath away from us, and to start a new covenant.

MARK 15:33

Was the darkness an eclipse of the sun?

Not possible. Jesus was crucified at the time of the Jewish Passover, which is always at full moon. At full moon, it is impossible to have a solar eclipse. Physically there is no adequate explanation of the darkness, other than that it is a supernatural sign at the time of mankind's darkest deed – killing the Son of God.

MARK 16:9-20

Why do we stop reading at Mark 16:8?

Most scholars agree that Mark's Gospel ends at chapter 16:8. The women run away terrified, not knowing what to think after being told that Jesus is risen. The ending provokes the question: are you able to see *who* Jesus is, *why* he came, and *what* it means to follow him?

Verses 9-20 of Mark chapter 16 appear to be attempts by later writers to add a fuller resurrection ending to Mark. However, the oldest manuscripts do not include this section, and its style and vocabulary are different from the rest of Mark. This does not mean that what is contained in this ending is made up. Most of the details also appear in the other Gospels. It just means that they were probably not in Mark's original.

Questions about Christian belief

How do you know that God exists?

- There are many philosophical and scientific arguments you can get involved in that might show that believing in God is rational and sensible. But these arguments lead to belief in some kind of creator, not specifically to the God of the Bible. It is usually much better to talk about Jesus and his claim to be God.

- We know God exists because he came to earth in Jesus. This is the core of Jesus' answer to Philip's question in John 14:8-9 (it's worth looking this up and reading it if the question arises).

- "Have you ever seen God?" "No, but I might have if I'd been born at the right time. If I had been alive 2000 years ago, and living in Palestine, I could have seen God."

- Jesus claimed to be God (eg: John 5:18; 20:28-29) and his actions bore out that claim. If you'd been there, you would have seen and heard him. Check out his claims as you read through Mark and come to *Christianity Explored*.

- Believing in God is not "the easy option". If he is God, then you must serve him as God.

Why should we believe what the Bible says?

- Try not to get involved in defending passages that can be interpreted in a number of different ways. The best place to start is with the reliability of what the Gospels teach about Jesus, and then go on to his teaching and claims on our lives.

- Historical evidence in the New Testament is confirmed at a number of points by non-Christian, historical writers – eg: Tacitus and Josephus – and also by archaeological evidence.

- The New Testament documents were written soon after the events they describe.

- This New Testament documentation is extensive, coming from as many as ten authors, eight of whom wrote independently of each other.

- The documents are historical in character as well as theological. They contain many verifiable details of the time and culture in which they were written.

- The text of these documents has come down to us intact from the era in which it was written.

- The writers were people who suffered and died for what they believed, and were also of very high moral standing. They believed in telling the truth. It is highly unlikely they would make up these stories, or even "imagine" them.

- The Gospels are less than complimentary to the disciples who wrote them – another sign that they were not made up.

- We have good historical reasons for trusting that what we read in the Gospels is an accurate account of what Jesus did, said and claimed for himself.

- The next step is to work out what you think of Jesus – everything else flows from that.

Don't all good people go to heaven?

- What is "good"? How "good" is good enough?

- Some of us are better than others, but no one meets God's standards (see Romans 3:23).

- We are not good, because our hearts are "sin factories" (Mark 7:21-22).

- People who rely on their goodness are deluded (Mark 10:17-22). There is always more we must do. We need rescuing.

- God is after friends, not "good" rebels. The issue is whose side you are on.

- The opposite is, in fact, true. "Good" people go to hell; bad people go to heaven. Those who think they are good, and rely on that, will be lost. Only those who know they are lost are able to receive forgiveness and eternal life from Christ.

Why would a good God send people to hell?

- God is utterly holy and good. His character is what decides right and wrong in the universe.

- God must judge everyone. He will judge fairly and well.

- Jesus is the most loving person who ever lived, but it is he who teaches most about the reality of hell. He does so because he knows it is real, and doesn't want us to suffer the inevitable consequences of our rebellion against God.

- Heaven and hell are defined by relationship. Heaven is enjoying all the good gifts of Father God, and being with him. Hell is the absence of his blessings – friendship, love, beauty, etc.

- God has judged his Son, Jesus, on the cross. He went through hell, so we don't have to!

- If we understood how holy God is, we would be asking the opposite question: how can God allow *anyone* into heaven?

If God forgives everything, does that mean I can do what I like?

◼ God's grace is utterly free. Shockingly, he will save even the worst kind of criminals you can think of.

◼ Jesus saved a condemned criminal who died on the cross next to him!

◼ If we properly understand how sinful we are, and how our sins have, literally, wounded God; and if we understand how amazing it is that Jesus died for us when we don't deserve it – then we want to live in a way that pleases him.

How can we be sure that there is life after death?

◼ People may come up with strange stories about "out-of-body experiences" but these prove nothing, and can lead to confusion.

◼ The Bible says that Jesus' resurrection is the pattern for our own resurrection (eg: 1 Corinthians 15:20).

◼ Who do you trust for accurate information about life beyond the grave? The person who has been there and come back.

◼ If Jesus has been raised from the dead, then we will certainly be raised from the dead, and we must look to Jesus' teaching for answers to the questions about what life beyond death will be like.

What about other religions?

◼ Sincerity is not truth. People can be sincerely wrong.

◼ If the different religions contradict each other (which they do at several major points), they cannot all be right.

◼ The question really is: has God revealed himself, and if so, how? Jesus claimed to be the unique revelation of God. He claimed to be God in the flesh. Are his claims valid? If Jesus is God, the other religions are wrong.

◼ Jesus claims he is the only way (John 14:6).

◼ Religions can do many good things – provide comfort, help, social bonding, etc. But they are man-made ideas about God, and generally teach that we must DO something to get right with God.

◼ Jesus claims that his teaching comes from God (John 8:28), and that his followers must abandon what they think they can do, and rely on what he has done on the cross to bring forgiveness and new life to them.

What about those who have never heard about Jesus?

◼ We can trust God to be just; he will judge people according to their response to what they know.

◼ Everyone has received some revelation, even if only from the created world (see Romans 1:18-19).

- Those who have had more revealed to them will be held more responsible (Matthew 11:20-24).

- You have heard, so you must do something about it – and leave the others to God, who will treat them fairly.

Isn't faith just a psychological crutch?

- There are different questions here, like: do I just believe because my parents were Christians? Or: do I believe because I have the need for some comfort from above? Or: do I believe because I have had this or that experience?

- If our faith is based purely on experience ("Christianity works for me"), then there is no way of arguing against this objection. It might work because it's true or because of my particular upbringing or conditioning.

- However, Christianity is based on objective historical events (the death and resurrection of Jesus), and invites people to investigate and test them. The truth of Christianity has nothing to do with our state of mind.

- The same could be applied to any belief – including atheism! (ie: I'm an atheist because my parents were; I have a deep need to be independent; I have had no experience.) None of this helps to establish whether belief in Christianity is based on truth or error.

Why does God allow suffering?

- We can't know for sure why God allowed evil into the world.

- Much suffering is a direct result of our own sinfulness (eg: that caused by drunkenness, greed, lust, etc.).

- But some is not (see John 9:1-3).

- All suffering results from the fallen nature of our world (see Romans 8:18-25).

- God uses suffering to discipline and strengthen his children (see Hebrews 12:7-11; Romans 5:3-5).

- God also uses suffering to wake people up so that they understand that there is a judgment coming to our pain-filled world (Luke 13:1-5).

- God knows our pain. He has done something about our suffering. Jesus suffered and died so that we could be forgiven and become part of the "new creation", where there will be no suffering. Jesus' death for us is the undeniable proof that God loves us.

Hasn't science disproved Christianity?

- Most people mean: "Hasn't the theory of evolution replaced creation and so disproved Christianity?" People usually are not talking about archaeology which, incidentally, backs up the Bible at almost every point.

- Start by asking what they mean by the question. They may have some specific point that needs addressing and that will require some research.

- Avoid having a technical discussion about evolution, carbon dating, etc.

- Ask what conclusion they are drawing from evolution. It may be a description of how life has appeared on earth (although you may want to dispute that!). But it does not answer the bigger questions: Who produced the amazing design and order that we see in the universe? For what purpose does the universe exist?

- Did the world come into being by chance? How God made the universe is not as important as the fact that he is the one who made it.

- Steer the conversation towards talking about God's existence (see above) and towards Jesus. If Jesus is God, it puts the creation/evolution debate in a completely different perspective.

If Jesus is God's Son, how can he be God too?

- Jesus lets himself be described as the "Son of God" – a term which can mean that he is the King of God's people, but can also be a claim that he is much more.

- Jesus acts in the New Testament in the way that God does in the Old Testament. He speaks as God speaks, and does things that only God can do (raises the dead, forgives sins, controls nature, etc.). His words and actions show that he is making a claim to be God.

- Christians do not believe that there are many gods, and that Jesus is just one of them. Christians believe that there is one God – who is a trinity. One God, three persons – the Father, the Son and the Holy Spirit in a relationship of love and service with each other.

- This is complex and hard to completely understand – but why would we expect to fully understand God anyway?

Why does God hate sex?

- He doesn't. He invented it and thinks it is beautiful, wonderful and powerful.

- God knows best how we work, and his pattern for sex – between a man and a woman in a committed, lifelong marriage – is the way he designed it to work best.

- Sex joins people together in a way that is more than physical. If we use sex in other ways, we will inevitably damage our ability to enjoy sex in the way it was intended.

- It may not appear damaging to enjoy this gift in other ways, but we must trust our Maker that it is.

Christians are hypocrites – so how can Christianity be true?

- The failure of many Christians to live according to their stated beliefs does not invalidate Jesus' claims to be God.

- The Bible says that Jesus alone is perfect, and it is honest about the failures and weakness of his followers. The disciples in Mark are constantly making mistakes.

- Jesus taught that there will always be false teachers and fakes (Mark 13:21-22) who pretend they are Christians but who are not. This is true today.

- Everyone is a hypocrite in some sense. But Jesus calls those who follow him to change and grow more like him. Don't be discouraged if you have met some Christians who are not yet perfect. They never will be this side of eternity.

Can we rely on Mark's Gospel?

This material is a copy of the notes found on page 62 of the group member's Handbook.

WHO? WHEN? WHY?

Mark was a close friend and companion of Peter, who was one of Jesus' disciples. Peter was an "apostle" (those specifically called to witness the life, death and resurrection of Jesus). Peter wrote two letters to the first-century Christian churches. In one of them he said: *"I will make every effort to see that after my departure* (ie: his death) *you will always remember these things."* (2 Peter 1:15). He was referring to the things he saw and knew about Jesus. He passed them on to others like Mark. Peter died in the mid 60s AD. The evidence suggests that Mark wrote his Gospel around that period.

No doubt Mark was influenced by Peter's desire for the news about Jesus to be told to others in later generations, so he wrote it down in a book. His opening sentence reveals the subject of his book: *"The beginning of the gospel about Jesus Christ, the Son of God."* (Mark 1:1).

Jesus died, rose again and returned to heaven around AD30. Mark wrote about 30 years later – well within the lifetime of those who lived through the events he recorded. So Mark had to write accurately. Any inconsistencies between what people saw and what he wrote would have discredited him.

HAS MARK'S BOOK CHANGED OVER TIME?

How different is Mark's original book from the book that we have today?

We don't have Mark's original to compare with the book we call Mark's Gospel. This is normal for ancient documents, since the original copy would have been written on material such as papyrus or parchment, which would eventually rot away.

For this reason historians assess the reliability of copies of an original by asking the following questions:

- How old are the copies?

- How much time has elapsed between the writing of the original document and the production of the copies that now exist?

- How many copies have been found?

The table below answers these questions for three widely-trusted historical works, and compares them with the New Testament (including Mark's Gospel).

	Date of original document	Date of oldest surviving copy	Approximate time between original and oldest surviving copy	Number of ancient copies in existence today
THUCYDIDES' HISTORY OF THE PELOPONNESIAN WAR	c. 431–400 BC	AD 900 plus a few late 1st-century fragments	1,300 years	73
CAESAR'S GALLIC WAR	c. 58–50 BC	AD 825	875 years	10
TACITUS' HISTORIES AND ANNALS	c. AD 98–108	c. AD 850	750 years	2
THE WHOLE NEW TESTAMENT	AD 40–100	AD 350	310 years	14,000 (approx 5,000 Greek; 8,000 Latin; 1,000 in other languages
(MARK'S GOSPEL)	(AD 60–65)	(3rd century)	(240 years or less)	

As the table shows, the oldest surviving copies of Mark were produced 240 years after his original (a comparatively small time) and an astonishing 14,000 copies exist today. So we can have great confidence that what we read is what Mark wrote.

Map

This map is included on page 64 of the group member's Handbook.

Mark tells us about the amazing things Jesus did and said. He also tells us where Jesus was at the time. Use the map to help you follow the story as Jesus travels around the country of Israel.

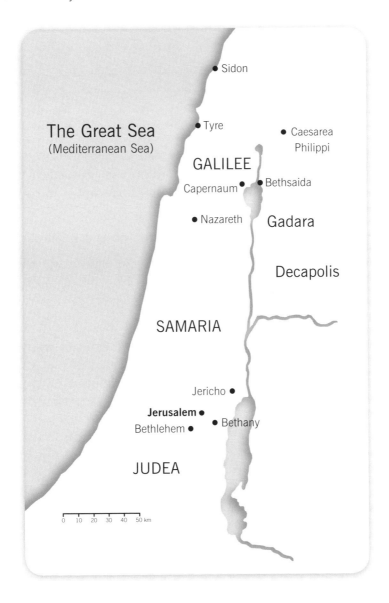

Acknowledgements...

This third edition of the *Christianity Explored* material was edited by Craig Dyer and Alison Mitchell, building on the original course material from the second edition, and the *Christianity Explored* DVD scripts written by Barry Cooper.

The first edition was developed by Rico Tice, Barry Cooper and Sam Shammas.

Literally hundreds of people have helped shape *Christianity Explored*, not least through the great feedback we have had from the thousands of leaders and guests who have used the course, and have been kind enough to give us their comments.

Special thanks to our review panel, who have commented on the revisions as we have gone along: Alex Bedford, Brad Byrd, Nicole Carter, Paul & Judy Chelson, David Childs, Karen Clark, Joanna Cook, Barry Cooper, Philip de Grey-Warter, Rosalind Groves, Lizzie Laferton, Philip Nye, Hugh Palmer, Gillian Pegler, Ian Roberts, Rico Tice, Tim Thornborough, David Williams, and Anne Woodcock.

Dashing designs by Steve Devane and André Parker.

Christianity Explored Ministries (CEM) aims to provide Christian churches and organisations world-wide with resources which explain the Christian faith clearly and relevantly from the Bible. CEM receives royalties from the sale of these resources, but is reliant on donations for the majority of its income. CEM is registered for charitable purposes in both the United Kingdom and the USA.

www.ceministries.org

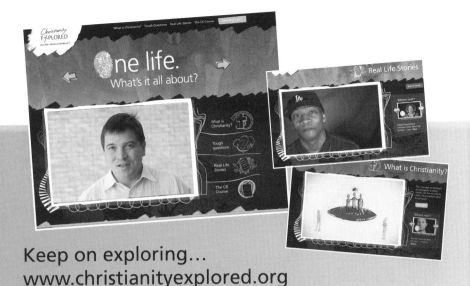

Keep on exploring...
www.christianityexplored.org

The *Christianity Explored* website helps non-Christians to explore Jesus' life and message in their own way and in their own time. It is equally useful for those thinking about coming on a course, and those who are going through *Christianity Explored*. It features:

- a visual outline explaining the gospel message, based on the Gospel of Mark
- real-life stories from people who've become Christians
- information about the *Christianity Explored* course
- short videos answering tough questions. These include:

  You can't trust the Bible, can you?

  Hasn't science shown that Christianity is wrong?

  If there is a God, why does he allow suffering?

  Wasn't Jesus just a great teacher?

  Why bother with church?

  Isn't believing in the resurrection ridiculous?

  How can a loving God send anyone to hell?

  Why are Christians so old-fashioned about sex?

  Surely it's arrogant to say your religion is the only right one?

  Doesn't becoming a Christian mean becoming boring?

Supporting downloads available from www.ceministries.org

- **Talk outlines** – Copies of the talks for the seven main sessions and for the day away are available as both pdfs and in Word format, so that you can personalise each talk with your own illustrations etc.

- **Visual aids** – A number of visual aids can be downloaded to show during the talks.

- **Extra illustrations** – If the suggested illustrations in the Leader's Guide don't suit your particular group or situation, you will find some alternatives available to download, which have been used by experienced *Christianity Explored* leaders. There are also suggestions for extra illustrations you may want to use to help your group understand key teaching points.

- **Feedback forms** – You may find it helpful to use a feedback form at the end of the course, both to find out how helpful the course was and also to discover what your group members would like to do next. A sample form is available on the website in a variety of designs and sizes. There is also a feedback form that you can give to leaders to get their comments and any suggestions for improvements.

- ***Christianity Explored* DVD trailers** – If you are going to show the *Christianity Explored* DVD during each session, then you may like to use a trailer as a way of inviting people to join. These can be downloaded from the website.

- **Logos for your own invitations** – If you are going to create your own printed invitations to the course, you can download copies of the *Christianity Explored* logo, which is available in a number of formats.

- **Other recommended resources** – Looking for something to help you or a course member with a particular issue? You'll find a huge range of recommendations, information and ideas on the website.

- **Evangelistic website** – you may find it helpful also to look at *Christianity Explored's* other website, which is designed for non-Christians. This includes testimonies, video clips of answers to common questions, and an outline of the gospel message. The web address is **www.christianityexplored.org**